THE
MIND
OF A
TRADER

Lessons in Trading Strategy
from the World's Leading Traders

ALPESH B. PATEL

FINANCIAL TIMES
PITMAN PUBLISHING

LONDON · HONG KONG · JOHANNESBURG
MELBOURNE · SINGAPORE · WASHINGTON DC

FINANCIAL TIMES MANAGEMENT
128 Long Acre, London WC2E 9AN
Tel: +44 (0)171 447 2000
Fax: +44 (0)171 240 5771
Website: www.ftmanagement.com

An imprint of Pearson Education Limited

First published in Great Britain in 1997

ISBN 0 273 63006 7

British Library Cataloguing in Publication Data
A CIP catalogue record for this book can be obtained
from the British Library.

5 7 9 10 8 6 4 2

Typeset by Pantek Arts, Maidstone, Kent
Printed and bound in Great Britain by
Biddles Ltd, Guildford and King's Lynn

*The Publishers' policy is to use paper manufactured
from sustainable forests.*

About the author

Alpesh Patel is a barrister-at-law who now runs his own successful derivatives fund, concentrating on traded equity options. As a barrister, Alpesh was involved in advising banks, building societies and pension funds on financial services. He has extensive experience of both the UK and US derivatives markets and holds equities in the UK, India, France and US. As former chairman of the University of London Finance Society, he lectured extensively on trading techniques. He is an associate of the Society of Technical Analysts and the Market Technicians Association (US) and a member of the Global Association of Risk Professionals. Alpesh also holds directorships in several Indian and English companies.

Alpesh Patel has a degree in philosophy, politics and economics from Oxford University and a degree in law from King's College, London. He is also the author of *Your Questions Answered: Money, Savings and Financial Planning* (1997).

If you would like to discuss anything in this book, the author's e-mail address is: alpesh-patel@msn.com

Contents

9 Brian Winterflood 185

(Managing Director, Winterflood Securities; former Director, County NatWest)
'I AM THE MOST FORTUNATE BLOKE YOU WILL EVER MEET'

10 Neal T. Weintraub 207

(Floor Trader; founder of the Center for Advanced Research in Computerized
Trading; author of *The Weintraub Day Trader* and *Tricks of the Floor Trader*)
'YOU CANNOT MASTER THE MARKET UNTIL YOU MASTER YOURSELF'

Brief Biographies of Interviewees

Bernard Oppetit

Banque Paribas, part of Groupe Paribas, is an international wholesale bank with a presence in over 60 countries. Groupe Paribas has total assets exceeding $269 billion. The Global Head of Equity Derivatives at Banque Paribas is Bernard Oppetit. He deals mainly with equity derivatives, options and index options, in all developed markets and a selected number of emerging markets such as Brazil, Argentina, Mexico, most of South East Asia and now Hungary and Poland.

Bill Lipschutz

Bill Lipschutz was Managing Director and Global Head of Foreign Exchange at Salomon Brothers at the end of the 1980s. Presently he is a Director of Trading at Hathersage Capital Management. Jack Schwager, in *The New Market Wizards* (1992), described Bill Lipschutz as 'Salomon Brothers' largest and most successful currency trader'. That is not surprising when you consider that a *single* Lipschutz trade might be measured in billions of dollars, and the resulting profits in tens of millions of dollars. Schwager estimated Bill's trading alone accounted for more than half a billion dollars profit for Salomon in the eight years he was there. That's the equivalent of $250,000 profit each and every trading day for eight years.

Pat Arbor

Pat Arbor is the Chairman of the Chicago Board of Trade (CBOT)– the world's largest and oldest futures and options exchange – a post he has held since 1993. Prior to the Chairmanship, he served on the Board of Directors from 1990 to 1993 and as Vice Chairman from 1987 to 1990. He has been a member of CBOT since 1965. He is also Chairman of the Board of Directors of the MidAmerican Commodity Exchange, an affiliate of the CBOT.

Jon Najarian

In 1989, Jon Najarian formed Mercury Trading, a designated primary market-maker responsible for maintaining a market in stocks for which it had been designated. Two years later it reported a return on capital of

415 per cent. Today it is the second most active market-maker on the – Chicago Board Options Exchange (CBOE). Mercury executes about half a million shares and 10000 options contracts – about $60 million worth of securities products. Chapter one of Rubenfeld's book, *The Super Traders* (1992), was devoted to him. He appears frequently on Financial News Network's weekly option report with Bill Griffith, and also appears on CNBC, WCIU, and Fox TV's 'Fox Thing in the Morning'. In 1994, Jon was elected to the CBOE Board of Directors and named Co-chairman of the marketing committee.

David Kyte

When only 24 years old David Kyte formed his own trading company with a mere £25,000. Today, at 36, he is the Chairman of Kyte Group Ltd and Kyte Broking Ltd, supervising gross profits running into millions. Kyte is also a member of the Board of Directors of LIFFE.

Phil Flynn

Phil Flynn is a Vice President of Alaron Trading. He 'trades anything'. Phil has been involved in the trading business since 1979, including a period handling Lind-Waldock's top customers.

Martin Burton

Martin Burton is the Managing Director of Monument Derivatives, the firm he formed in 1991. He became a member of the London Stock Exchange at 21 years old and a partner of Bisgood Bishop at 22. He established Monument after four years as Managing Director at Citibank, where he was responsible for all trading in UK and European Equities and Derivatives, prior to which he was at County NatWest where he established the derivatives operation.

Paul RT Johnson Jr

Paul RT Johnson Jr is a member of the Board of Directors of the Chicago Board of Trade and is a floor trader at CBOT, after a spell in the early 1980s at the Chicago Mercantile Exchange. Paul is also Senior Vice President at ING Securities, Futures & Options Inc., and President of LSU Trading Company. He trades bonds, mainly five and ten year, and bond options, although much of his income stems from his partnership in his own brokerage business.

Brian Winterflood

Brian Winterflood is the Managing Director of Winterflood Securities, established in May 1988. They provide a jobbing service (creating and providing dealing prices) in over half the companies quoted on the London Stock Exchange, the complete list of AIM (Alternative Investment Market) stocks, 90 per cent of SEAT stocks, plus the whole of the gilts market. It is now a subsidiary of the Close Brothers Group, the second largest 'quoted' Merchant Bank. There are only three major wholly English Houses left in London: BZW, NatWest and Winterflood Securities. He was formerly a Director of County NatWest.

Neal T. Weintraub

Neal Weintraub is a pit trader (local) as well as an off-floor computer trader. Perhaps more significantly, Weintraub is an educator and commodity trading advisor. He is the founder of the Center for Advanced Research in Computerized Trading and conducts seminars on day-trading and international hedging. Weintraub teaches at De Paul University, the Chicago Mercantile Exchange, and has been on the staff of the Chicago Board of Trade where he was instrumental in introducing the Treasury Bond Options contract. Most of Weintraub's students are professional floor personnel and career traders, from both the US and around the world. The *Wall Street Journal* has featured his Pivot Point technique and he is frequently quoted in the trade press. Indeed, in conjunction with TradeWind Publishing, Neal has recently launched the *Weintraub Day Trader* software which incorporates Pivot Point analysis. Neal Weintraub is the author of *The Weintraub Day Trader* (1991) and *Tricks of the Floor Trader* (1996). He is a member of the MidAmerican Commodity Exchange and clears his trades through Goldenberg and Hehmeyer at the Chicago Board of Trade.

In loving memory of Dada, (Rambhai Umedbhai)

&

To my family – always with me:

Sushilaba

Mummy & Papa
(Ramilabhen) (Bipinchandra)

Janak Kaka	*Hashmita Auntie*	*Sakufoi*	*Yashvin Kaka*	*Hansa Auntie*
Archana	*Nishaan*	*Priyen*	*Nishika*	*Sunaina*

Selina

Or else to learnéd families
of disciplined he comes again,
tho' such a birth as that on earth
is harder to obtain

And there united with the mind
from the body he had left behind,
from that point onward strives
to win perfection's prize

(Bhagavad Gita, 6: 42, 43 trans. by Geoffrey Parrinder. One World, 1974.)

Preface

The mental processes leading to trading excellence and profit are described within the covers of this book from the mouths of those who experience, live, breathe and love the markets. What do top trading strategies and minds have in common? How can the reader use this information to his or her own advantage and profit? I do not want a single trading reader to close any chapter and feel 'what relevance does this have to me?'.

The naïve believe there is a secret to trading success, and they search for it, but in the wrong places, such as expensive trading programs. With experience they realize that the only secret to success is hard work and talent, and they stop looking for any other secret. Finally, with wisdom, they stumble across the secret to trading success without even realizing it. Any secret is the knowledge possessed by the few. The secret to trading success is in this book. That secret is a frame of mind, a way of seeing things.

Trading is viewed by many as seductively easy until they start losing, until they become one of the 80–90 per cent that do not last a year in the profession. Trading success is difficult. Better to learn from the mistakes of the successful and avoid your own, than to become a loss-making statistic. Successful traders need not only successful trading rules, but also a successful trading mind. Having successful trading rules is only half the picture; knowing how to achieve the mentality to implement them provides the full picture.

Throughout the book trading strategies are placed within a psychological context, demonstrated through the experience of top traders. I seek to get behind the mind of the trader and examine how he implements his winning strategies. What great map, what unusual perspective has he been granted that permits his view to be uniquely profitable? After all, the lawyer's job is to get the other person, whatever his occupation, to tell his story so that anyone and everyone can easily understand it. However, being a trader myself has meant that I too have experienced the problems, frustrations and questions which are addressed in this book. I have tried to be your collective mouthpiece. I believe I have managed to get to the root of popular trading difficulties not effectively addressed elsewhere. For instance, how do I know if I am cutting a loss short or if I am cutting a loss which could be a potential profit?

Rather than providing an over-simplistic, unhelpful and sprawling question-and-answer format that is heavy on biography and history, I have chosen to incorporate my eminent interviewees' responses into digestible, focused sections within a coherent study of techniques. There is explanation and expansion wherever needed and not merely at the end of a chapter or hidden in a conclusion.

If you prefer your trading books to be rambling accounts of trades placed decades ago in markets that no longer exist, with a few impoverished paragraphs of advice and little focus on the reader, then this book is not for you. You will find this book written in an accessible, direct and useful style, containing descriptions of what these leading traders do so well and how you yourself can improve your trading and, ultimately, make more money.

The Interviewees

In the latter half of the twentieth century there exists a political and economic system that holds dominion over all others. It is the aspired destination of states yet to reach it, and the sanguine attainment of those which have. Success within this system is defined by the accumulation of capital through the trading of commodities. This system is Capitalism. Although they are more popularly known as traders, the individuals interviewed in this book are skillful and accomplished capitalists.

This is the broadest collection of traders ever assembled. They come from the world's three leading trading cities: New York, Chicago and London. Not surprisingly, what they have to teach has universal appeal and a surprising consistency yet originality. Introduced for the first time are the concepts of 'dynamic analysis', 'progressive trading', 'pyramid information', 'the Swiss method', and many others.

These ten men have significantly improved my own trading. Not only have I learnt things I never knew before, despite having read virtually every trading book on the market, equally importantly they have confirmed many things I have discovered myself. I hope and believe you will get as much from this book as I did researching and writing it.

Alpesh Bipin Patel
Chicago and London 1997

Acknowledgments

First, I owe great thanks to all those who agreed to be interviewed for this book. All of them are extremely busy men and I greatly appreciate the time they spared. Theirs was a sincere desire to pass on knowledge so that up and coming traders might benefit.

Thank you Yashvin kaka for initially sowing the seed which eventually grew into this book. I think few people will be more happy or more proud to see this project successfully completed. Many thanks to Saku auntie for typing various parts of the book at very short notice, despite her own busy schedule. As ever she was selfless and generous, but never taken for granted.

Great thanks are owed to Selina, who will be my wife by the time she reads this. Thank you so very much for all the proof reading and typing in the midst of wedding preparations. Never once did you put yourself before this project. Always will I remember.

I would also like to thank every other member of my family; each one has expressed an interest in the book throughout and that has provided immense support to me. Since my first trade at the age of 12, I have been provided with a nurturing environment in which exploration of all areas of finance was encouraged. Each member of my family embodies the entrepreneurial spirit. They expect no thanks but deserve from me more gratitude than I can ever grant.

Thanks are also owed to Anand Tharamaratnam and Sheila Sagayam for their initial introduction to Amwedhkar Jethoe, whom I also thank, as this triggered a series of events culminating in the first interview.

Thanks, too, to everyone who proof-read various chapters at various stages.

Finally, I wish to express sincere thanks to Richard Stagg and the team at FT/Pitman Publishing for their prompt and attentive support at each stage of the publication process. I have been very fortunate to have found such a superlative publisher.

Introduction

Jack Wigglesworth

Chairman, LIFFE

This is a fascinating book from which the reader can gain an insight into how the best in their field today succeed in an activity which is as old as human societies. Over the centuries trading has been an activity involving goods strategic to human needs – grains, metals, foods, minerals, animal and vegetable products required for releasing energy or making clothing and so on. Some of these goods have had qualities which caused them to be used as a medium of exchange or a store of value, which meant they were used as money and attracted the interest of, and led to varying degrees of control by, the sovereign bodies of the jurisdictional areas.

Those who have made trading these products, rather than using them, a profession have often been regarded as a breed apart, envied, pilloried, taxed more highly than those merely using the products, expelled by authorities who wanted a monopoly for themselves or privileged citizens.

Traders work best when in close proximity with others in central markets, where there is transparency of price formation, easy access to information on others' activity and good settlement and delivery mechanisms with safeguards provided by the market as a whole to protect any one of them from the insolvency of another. From the twenty-first century it may be that all these best attributes of markets may be available in cyberspace or virtually as technology advances, but all those interviewed in this book are based in one of the great trading market cities, such as London, Chicago and New York. Such cities, like Amsterdam, were typically at the heart of mercantilist trading nations, with good communication and access to the rest of the world by ship. Exploration, conquest and empire-building was associated with the quest for the products of such market traders and the protection of the trading routes. Whatever the different techniques of the successful individual traders in this book, it is clear that the best have a sort of sixth sense which cannot be learned from any academic course. Keeping their ear to the ground and having all the same information as others, they have a sense of timing and the guts to go for it in a contrarian fashion, which is by definition abnormal. That is why words used to describe them such as 'speculator', have a pejorative sense in common usage. Speculators or traders are essential to provide liquidity in a market where others can achieve their non-trading aims.

During the 1997 UK general election campaign, a lady, interviewed by the BBC, said that a single currency in Europe was needed to stop the foreign exchange speculators. This attitude, common among many people, including politicians, shows how the emotion around the connotation of a word can prevent consideration of important technical factors. In this case it hindered consideration of whether a single currency across many different countries, without a single government, fiscal policy, or labour mobility across the region to match that in the United States, or a robust system of transferring resources from rich to poor regions can possibly work if the same rate of interest has to be imposed on countries with tight as well as on countries with loose fiscal policies. History has shown that when 'speculators' made money in forex markets was when another speculator, usually a government, was trying to hold a price untenable in the market.

As the twentieth century ends it is hard to realize how great were the swings in climate for traders. The century began with the UK at the height of its imperial fortune and the centre of world trade and finance. There was no significant tax or regulation on traders. Merchant bankers, traders on the Stock Exchange and commodity markets in London were making, and losing, huge fortunes. In the United States massive speculation was rampant, with the industrialization of the country led by the developers of the steel industry. The Chicago grain and other produce exchanges were established. The First World War limited the activities of traders (as did the Second) but the power of banks, with their fingers in so many businesses, led to the problem of protecting depositors from their other activities and the start of formal regulation in the 1920s and 1930s, splitting banking from securities activities and regulating commodity and securities investment. The peak of regulation and demarcation between services provided by different professions was seen in the 1950s to 1970s. In the UK, individuals as traders died out in the post-Second World War years, largely because of high personal taxation and a tax regime which encouraged individuals to invest through institutions such as pensions funds and insurance companies.

At the end of the Bretton Woods era, the breakdown of which led to the growth of financial futures and OTC derivatives, enterprising individuals and traders were a rare species. Indeed, when we proposed the setting up of LIFFE we were told that it would not work as, in contrast to Chicago, there were no individual traders in the UK to become the 'locals' in the Exchange, which would flounder through lack of liquidity if the only members were institutions!

With the lower personal tax regime and reduced incentives to save institutionally of the 1980s, together with the deregulation, the markets saw traders and entrepreneurs come out of the woodwork in spades, like seeds sprouting in the desert after the first shower for decades. The City of London has survived all the difficulties, including 40 years of exchange controls, and is now, at the end of the century, the undoubted dealing centre for trading international commodity and financial instruments.

The importance of traders is evidenced most obviously by the outstanding success of London's derivative exchanges in recent years: the IPE has developed the main world crude oil benchmark in its Brent Crude contract; the LME has seen phenomenal growth and dominates the world in non-ferrous and non-precious metals trade; LIFFE, with its unsurpassed international membership, has risen from its birth in late 1982 to be the world's leading international futures and options exchange, trading a far broader range of instruments than any other – futures and options on money market instruments, bonds, soft and agricultural commodities, equity index products and traded options on ordinary shares – in seven major currencies. LIFFE's growth has been in excess of 40 per cent per annum compound, placing it, in terms of turnover, second only to the Chicago Board of Trade.

Such growth illustrates the insatiable demand from businesses all around the globe for the products offered, which, when used in the proper way, can give a company a competitive advantage against other businesses in the same industry as well as taking the benefits of secure future delivery of essentials to the man in the street and protection for him against price fluctuations. His pension is more secure and his mortgage can be at a fixed rate. These are the benefits available to all of us because traders are there to provide the essential liquidity to the markets.

Jack Wigglesworth
Chairman, LIFFE
April 1997

1

Bernard Oppetit

'WE WERE MAKING
A LOT OF MONEY VERY
CONSISTENTLY.'

TRADING TOPICS

- Bottom-up analysis

- Dynamic analysis

- The 'Swiss method': objectivity and neutrality

- Risk and probability analysis

- Optimal portfolio diversification

- Characteristics of great traders

- Stops

Banque Paribas, part of Groupe Paribas, is an international whole-sale bank with a presence in over 60 countries. Groupe Paribas has total assets exceeding $269 billion. The Global Head of Equity Derivatives at Banque Paribas is Bernard Oppetit, a slim, tall and pensive Frenchman.

In both nationality and geography, Banque Paribas sets itself apart from other major banks; it is French, and in London is located in the West End, not the City (*vive la difference!*). The French, as they have a tendency to do, have brought native elegance with them. Marble stairs spill down, forming an arch from the first floor to the lobby. Crystal chandeliers emit a dim light, adding to the sophistication of the interior. The temptation is too great to resist the cliché: the interior is chic and there is a *je ne sais quoi* about it. The conference rooms, together with numerous mementos of completed projects, have pictures of famous French landmarks – Sacré Coeur, Champs Elysées, Tour Eiffel. Even the water is Evian and Perrier.

Bernard Oppetit deals mainly with equity derivatives, options and index options, in all developed markets and a selected number of emerging markets such as Brazil, Argentina, Mexico, most of South East Asia and now Hungary, Russia and Poland. 'We have customers' business and proprietary business. The customer business is for the most part in index products. We act as a dealer. We also have quite a big proprietary business which is more a single security business.'

The life and times of Bernard Oppetit

'I started working at Paribas 17 years ago; fresh out of school. I started in Paribas's Technology department. It did not last very long. This was the very early ages of IT, way before PCs appeared on every desk. I was then involved in merchant banking for Paribas in Paris from 1982 to 1987. In this capacity I was working on a big transaction with an insurance company, of which we owned 25 per cent and the rest was held by the public. There was a bidding war for this company and between the beginning and the end of the bidding war, the stock was up 400 per cent. This was in 1986; this was when I said to myself, "I should be in risk arbitrage; I should be looking for the next take-over target." I moved to New York in 1987 was appointed head in 1990 and I remained there until 1995.

'Then I became the head of the group which then expanded to a desk in London and a desk in Asia. We were making a lot of money very consistently; we never sought any kind of publicity because we never wanted to raise any money; it was always Paribas's capital. At the time my name was in the press quite a lot in New York.

'I was looking at trading special situations such as mergers, take-overs, bankruptcies, all sorts of restructuring etc., with a very open mind and trading in equity, options, bonds in almost everything. There was one very important caveat – which was that we always had a bottom-up approach. There was never a top-down view of the world, it was always company-specific. There is something going on very specifically in this company, this is what is going on, this is what this guy wants to do and that guy wants to do. It was things like that, never a macro approach based on interest rates or currencies or macro-trends.

'I had been doing that for eight years and two years ago I was asked to head the equity derivatives operation in London, worldwide in fact. I accepted because I was able to remain involved in the risk arbitrage business. I have responsibility for over 40 traders in New York, London, Paris, Singapore, Tokyo and Hong Kong, who are for the most part option traders.'

Risk arbitrage

'Traditionally risk arbitrage was understood as involving merger and take-over arbitrage and this is how we started, but what we call risk arbitrage now is not only that, but also various plays on distressed securities, various plays on all sorts of corporate events that can lead to a price movement and that we can take advantage of.

'For example, right now, which is not particularly take-over related, you will have heard about the American tobacco litigation cases. There is a lot going on there in court and in Congress. There is a lot of action from the companies themselves, basically it is a battlefield. You have on the one hand the tobacco companies which are trying to protect themselves from the risk of potential responsibility and on the other hand regulators, the government, the courts, and interest groups formed of various ex-smokers.

'The outcome of this battle is going to affect the market value of these stocks by tens of billions of dollars. So there is a lot of money to be made or lost if you get that right. A typical risk arbitrage trade we would do is to look at this with a very open mind, studying everything that could happen and trade tobacco stocks, or other stocks for that matter, from that angle.

'It can be directional. If we think the next battle will be won by tobacco companies we can go long tobacco companies. If we think the next battle is going to be won by the other party we can go short. If we think that the outcome of the next battle is going to send the stock sharply in one direction or another we can buy the straddle. [Long a call and put option to benefit from a price move in either direction. See Trading Appendix 1 on options.] On the contrary, if we think that nothing much is going to happen or that it is too expensive, we can sell the straddle. We have a very open mind; there is absolutely no potential trade we would not play. So that is typically the kind of trade I have been doing for ten years now.'

Bottom-up analysis: becoming an expert to gain the edge

The approach which Bernard Oppetit highlights above involves him examining a company and becoming an expert on it. His primary focus is the individual company. The opposite strategy would be top-down, involving first an analysis of a country, or a sector, and then eventually the consequences for a company. Oppetit will spend hours researching, trying to get into the minds of the company's managers, shareholders, employees, bankers, creditors, debtors and of course those who trade the company's shares. He is looking to calculate what is going to happen next that could affect the price. Such total focus and accumulation of expertise is likely to give him a natural edge over those relying on secondary sources of analysis.

The NorthWest Airlines case study

'We did a play on NorthWest Airlines; it was in 1993. In 1989 there was an LBO of the airline. Then the airline industry went through a terrible time. They collectively lost billions and billions of dollars, and NorthWest did very poorly as well. At that time the balance sheet of NorthWest airlines revealed a lot of bank debts and a relatively small bond issue. (I think it was 500 million dollars versus a balance sheet of six or seven billion dollars, the rest was bank debt.) Because it went through a second very tough time, NorthWest threatened bankruptcy. It did some tough negotiating with the banks and its employees, its suppliers, basically anybody who had something to lose if NorthWest went bust.

'NorthWest started to extract some concessions from them. They extracted a lot of concessions from the banks, who waved interest and extended security, and from Boeing by delaying payment for the planes. In order to get that they had to be adamant that they were on the brink of bankruptcy. Every day there would be reports in the papers saying, "we are going bankrupt". That's why the bonds started trading lower and lower. Eventually the bonds traded 10 cents on the dollar.

'My analysis was that they would not go bankrupt. I felt they were trying to scare everybody. It was clearly in their interests to do that. It was just a ploy to extract concessions from all these other parties. For me there was no point in doing anything with the bonds because it was small. So instead, at this point, I started buying NorthWest debt. Of course we might have lost a lot, but we believed we might make even more. Our analysis was that NorthWest was bluffing.

'Once they got the concessions everything miraculously went back to normal. They started publishing good numbers and the bonds went back up to par and so we made four or five times our money. The company then went public and is still doing very well.

'There is a lot of fundamental analysis which goes into that. In modern fundamental analysis there is the need to understand the dynamics, especially with such a special situation.

'A very similar case was Eurodisney. With them there was a convertible bond and when they went into trouble they, in the same way as NorthWest, made all sorts of terrible noises as to how things were going badly. They screwed the bank, shareholders and everybody else, but they did not touch the bonds, and the same kind of thing happened. That was a very good trade for us as well.'

'In the case of Eurodisney, the fact that this bond was convertible, i.e. a derivative instrument, probably helped a lot in getting this mispricing because many derivatives traders do not know the underlyings, and the people who trade the underlyings do not understand derivatives. If you understand both, you start with a huge advantage.'

The benefits of such concentrated, strategic thinking are clear. They provide the ability to see something others have not and to profit from that knowledge. Of course that will not always be the case. It can be that there is nothing that the others have missed or that there is no hidden agenda. Furthermore, hard work alone will not provide insight. Insight is best nurtured through experience. A good way to develop the necessary experience is to follow company stories in newspapers.

- You will need to identify all the players, and what they are saying. A player is anyone with more than minimal influence, including a group, for example a union can be a player.
- Next, identify what they have to gain by saying what they are saying. What are the motives and hidden agendas. Never take people at their word when their livelihoods are at stake.
- Who has the most to lose?
- Who has the most to gain?
- What would be each party's first-, second- and third-choice outcomes?
- What leverage and influence can the parties exert to steer events in their preferred direction?
- How would each party react to each outcome? If one individual behaves in one way, how will the others react and what will the consequences be?

Thinking through corporate events like this is a skill which takes time to develop. However, it can very much add to the fun and interest of trading, particularly if you enjoy chess, poker or politics! Finally, remember, for Oppetit, prices are moved by corporate events. It is the case that corporate events are shaped by individuals with power. Power is the ability to influence. Therefore in following the chain of causation leading to a price move, your initial starting question is, 'who has influence?'. Always remember that many people have influence in relation to a company and a particular situation.

Always keep an open mind. As Oppetit describes in his stories, at times the courts are the power brokers. With NorthWest it was many people, including the banks. Power and influence are fluid. That makes your task of following the likely consequences of corporate actions more difficult and more interesting.

Dynamic analysis

Bernard Oppetit introduced a fascinating concept that I have not previously encountered to describe his method of analysis.

'I think fundamental analysis is very important, but so is what I call "dynamic analysis". You try to understand what the hell is going on with this company, who is trying to do what, why, how much and when. There is always a story and you have to understand the story.'

Bernard Oppetit's point is that corporate events do not occur in a vacuum. There is cause and effect to every company event. It is an understanding of this context and environment that is essential.

'Applied to stocks, I think 99 per cent of technical analysis is garbage, although that is less true for things such as currencies and most commodities, indices, interest rates. There I think technical analysis is very important. It is very difficult there because there is not just one right way of doing it, and even if you do it badly it can be better than not doing it at all. But again, it is important also to figure out the story – who is trying to do what. The actors, instead of being the banks, the company's suppliers and shareholders, are likely to be governments, supply and demand and producers.

> *'There is always a story and you have to understand the story.'*

'There are hundreds of ways to skin a cat and you can make money from technical analysis alone. Personally I don't know how to do it. I am sure it can be done.'

Dynamic analysis is the name Oppetit gives to the type of analysis he did with NorthWest. He wants to know the 'story'. What are the motives? Where is the influence (i.e., who are the actors)? The analysis is 'dynamic' presumably because the situation will not be static. He is not examining last year's profit and loss accounts or the balance sheet. There is a live situation which could alter dramatically in a relatively short period of time and have significant repercussions for the stock price.

However, dynamic analysis is not always the most appropriate analytical tool. Bernard Oppetit varies his analysis depending on the type of trade and situation in question. This is very important if you trade different types of market and are examining different time-frames. For instance, looking at an intra-day trade in a liquid market, technical analysis would be more appropriate than fundamental analysis. If, on the other hand, one were looking to take a view over several months based on a country's economic prospects, fundamental analysis would be more suitable than technical analysis.

'I do a lot of different types of trade. Convertible arbitrage, for example, is something I do. It is more a pure derivatives strategy, which can involve buying implied volatility and selling historical volatility. That may involve more technical analysis. For risk arbitrage it would be a very different kind of trade.'

What is the other guy thinking?

In any competitive environment, such as trading, you must think through why things are as they are at any moment in time. Why is the price what it is? Why is volume low today? Why is the bank buying this company's shares? Why is this other bank selling them? Why has the managing director bought extra shares? If you do not understand what is around you, you are unlikely to know why or whether things will change. Whether you are seeking a change in price

'There is no doubt in my mind that you are better off doing the opposite of what the crowd is doing.'

tomorrow or hoping for the price to be the same tomorrow, unless you comprehend today, you cannot understand tomorrow.

'Something I would always ask myself is, "do I know enough about what I am trying to do? Do I know more than the other guy? Why does he do what he is doing? If I am buying, why is he selling? What does he think?" If I cannot figure out what is in his mind I am not going to be very comfortable. It is a way to be contrarian. There is no

THE MIND OF A TRADER

doubt in my mind that you are better off doing the opposite of what the crowd is doing. But it can be difficult to measure what the consensus is doing. On the other hand, the consensus can be right as well, for example the US market has been bullish and the consensus has been correct.

'I have to understand what the other side has in mind, and what is in my mind that is not in theirs. It can be very simple; for example they may simply not think in terms of implied volatility. If I think I am buying cheap implied volatility and the other side looks at it differently, then I will know why they are doing it. If I still think I am doing the right thing then that is good enough.'

This sort of comprehensive thought process is also a good tool in risk management. It ensures you have not missed anything, and you know exactly why you have placed a trade. Consequently, when you place the trade you should do so with more confidence and with a clearer picture of your expectations. Whatever happens once the trade is executed, you will have a good idea of why it happened and be able to act with more certainty than would otherwise have been the case.

The Swiss method of viewing an open position: objectivity and neutrality

I call Bernard Oppetit's method of viewing an open position the 'Swiss method' because at all times he is very conscious that he must place emotion to one side and be objective and neutral.

As every trader knows, at the moment a trade is executed, everything is different. That is the point at which it becomes real, no longer digits on a screen and numbers in an account. Now expectation is joined by anticipation. The brain is joined by the heart. Reason is joined by emotion. You exchange detachment for attachment.

When you have an open position and you are looking to close it, you will either have a profit or a loss. The emotions relating to each are quite different. For instance, when sitting on a loss many traders experience hope that the position will turn around because they fear and deny that it may not. It is for you to recognize these emotions and to discard them. Your judgment has to be based on detached reasons relating to your analysis of the company.

How you behave once you have an open position is all-important. Without clear thinking you could exit too soon or too late. Your key concern with an open position is timing your exit. Of course there are times when you are deciding whether to add to a position, but generally you are concerned with exit. With an open position you are concerned with closing the position. In order to do that an open position requires an open mind.

'The key is to be intellectually honest. You have to think of every day as a clean slate. You've got to forget about your loss or how much you paid. You have to treat each day as a completely new day. You have to start every day with a blank page. Mark to market should be the rule so you start each day afresh. There is no expected profit or loss on the books so you have to start from scratch each morning.

> *'I think emotions are far more important than brains in being a good trader.'*

'You have to be very, very honest with yourself. You must not kid yourself. Whether you have a position that is underwater or you are sitting on a huge profit, you have to look at it in exactly the same way. That is the main reason why people lose money in the market. I am very glad that that's the case because if it wasn't the case, it would be very difficult for people like me to consistently make money in the market.'

As Bernard Oppetit notes, honesty in examining a position is impeded by emotions surrounding the positions.

'I think emotions are far more important than brains in being a good trader. And in emotions this is the tough part, to look at positions in a completely neutral way, even though you may be completely destroyed or, on the contrary, you may have made millions.'

Facing a loss
When sitting on a paper loss a trader will indubitably experience immense pressure and fear.

'It is very important to experience this fear to ensure you do not end up in that situation again. Fear is also a bad thing in that it will affect your judgment, in the same way elation would affect your judgment. You have to take a very neutral approach.'

So, experience the fear when faced with a loss, do not deny it. But use the fear as a means of loss-prevention in future, not as a cause of ever increasing losses. When looking at a new price you do not focus on the fear of how much you have lost, or the hope it may turn around.

'You have to ask if you are a buyer at this new price. If you didn't own it already, would you buy it? If the answer is no, then I sell it. You have to look at the position with an open mind and ask if you would put it on today if you did not already have it. If new information came in while I had an open position, I would change my expectations. But you have to be honest with yourself. It is a question of attitude. It is an easy trap to fall into to kid yourself that you are holding on to something because you believe things have changed and it will now rise. It comes back to being honest with yourself.'

Handling a profit

As well as hope, another damaging emotion surrounding open positions which prevents an honest analysis, is that an unrealized profit may vanish.

> *'Whether I get out at a profit or loss does not matter.'*

'It is a cliché that you cut your losers and ride your winners – but it is very true. Most people and many traders do the opposite. There is a desire to take profits, sometimes encouraged by accounting rules. Many people look at their unrealized gains as non-existent. They think taking profit is making real profit and it is unreal before then. They feel taking a loss is an admission of being wrong.'

Again, this emotional attitude to profits has to be eradicated. Instead of focusing on whether he was right or wrong, Bernard Oppetit focuses on his expectations regarding a position, in order to maintain objectivity.

'If what I had expected to happen does not happen, then I know to get out. Whether I get out at a profit or loss does not matter. As soon as I realize my scenario was wrong I get out. Another easy case is when everything I expected happened, so I take my profits. Those are the two easy cases, and everything in between is difficult.'

What Bernard Oppetit is discussing is that all open positions have to be viewed objectively. That means you have to focus on certain questions and reasons and ignore others. You need to focus on:

- Has what you expected to happen, happened?
- Are you a buyer or a seller at this price?
- Is the probability of what you expected to occur still the same as when you placed the trade?

You have to ignore:

- How much of a loss you are sitting on.
- How much of a profit you are sitting on.
- How much you paid for the position.
- Hope that the position may turn around.

Trading: art and science

'I think to have a scientific training is good in that respect, although sometimes it can be misleading because in the markets there is no truth like there is in physics or mathematics. However, being used to thinking about things scientifically helps. The scientist has to be honest with himself. There is no fudging around. If the result of an experiment is a flop, then it is a flop, there is no messing around. Facts are facts, you cannot reshape them.'

However, despite all the objectivity, trading is not mechanical, there remains room for skill. After all, do not the Swiss make beautiful watches?

'At the same time trading is far more an art than a science. When a trader makes a decision he never fully knows why he is making that decision. You have to think about your trade and the market night and day, but at some point you want to pull the trigger. You have thought of hundreds of things over the previous few days, so that if I ask you, "why are you buying or why are you selling?", you will not be able to give a good answer. You may be able to give a few reasons, but that will not be the full answer. The entire message is everything you have thought about over the last three days, and that would take three days to explain. A lot of it is subconscious. You do not really know why you are pulling the trigger. To that extent it is more an art than a science, because you cannot fully demonstrate why you are doing what you are doing. In options there is a lot of science and it requires you to be both a scientist and an artist. That is why I guess it is so difficult to find good derivatives traders.'

Great traders tend to be risk-averse

The public perception of traders, propagated by trading scandals, is that they are attracted to wild risks and take massive gambles. Of all the traders I interviewed for this book, not one claimed to be risk-loving.

'I am very risk-averse. I would definitely take the certainty of making $10,000 dollars rather than the 10 per cent chance of making $100,000. In terms of economics, my personal utility function is very much concave.'

> *'You do not need to risk a lot to profit a lot.'*

When we speak of risk in trading we are of course discussing price volatility. Price volatility cannot be discussed without an idea of probability. The probability of a stock's price reaching your target can be derived from the historic price volatility of the particular stock. Consequently, risk, price volatility and probability go hand in hand. Good traders wait until the probability of a favorable move is the greatest and the risk of an unfavorable move the lowest. Moreover, unlike non-professional traders, the great trader knows that risk and reward are not always directly proportional. There are very low risk and yet high reward trades.

'The important thing is to look at risk in a rational way, and an imaginative way. A good trader knows how and when to take risk and how and when to avoid risk. There are risks which should be taken and risks which should not be taken. The game is to distinguish between the two. You do not need to risk a lot to profit a lot. There are a lot of trades where you can make a lot of money that are not particularly risky. You may have to invest a lot of your time to do research and discover what is going on, but the actual money you invest may not be at much risk.'

'There is a joke about an economics professor who is walking in New York with a friend. His friend notices a $100 bill on the sidewalk and points to the bill and says, "look professor, a $100 bill". The economics professor replies, "no that cannot be so, if that was a $100 bill somebody would have picked it up already". Still I believe there are opportunities to make money with very little risk.'

Analyzing risk and probability

So, how does Bernard Oppetit analyze risk and probability when he examines a position?

'Even though I know I will get out after a certain loss, I consider the amount I have risked as the whole amount invested. Also, I look to see what percentage probability there is of a certain percentage rise and I compare that to the risk I am taking. I would look at some kind of distribution of possible outcomes, such as a 50 per cent chance of doing something special or a 50 per cent chance of doing nothing in particular, or a 50 per cent chance of a small loss against a 50 per cent chance of a great gain. There has to be some idea of the distribution of outcomes.'

What Bernard Oppetit does when analyzing a potential trade is to consider at risk the whole amount he is trading with. This is even if he knows that he will exit the position if the price falls by, say, 15 per cent and therefore he would only risk losing 15 per cent of his stake. He then examines the reward. He measures reward by examining the probabilities of various outcomes. One can only gain an idea of the reward if one examines the probability of it occurring.

Bernard Oppetit would then compare the risk with the reward. For instance, an options position opened with $10,000 would place $10,000 at risk. To get an idea of his risk and reward ratio, Bernard Oppetit would then examine the likely outcomes and their probabilities. This would give him some idea of the reward he may get for the risk he is taking. (If he were being very mathematical, he would sum the products of all the outcomes and their corresponding probabilities, and compare this figure to the amount risked.)

Money management

Good risk analysis and management is not only about volatility and probability, it is also about good money management.

'You have to have good money management. You have to ensure you are not going to be hopelessly underwater. You can have rules like maximum drawdown or value at risk or limits. You can also have your own internal rules like "this is too much money to lose". You must have that in your mind and that you are not going to risk more than that at any one time. You have to make sure you are left in the game. That is very important. Once this is clearly established, you need to feel that things can very quickly go wrong.'

In devising a money management plan, you would consider the following:

- What is the most money I will risk on any single trade at any one time, that is, what is too much to be lost? What amount must I avoid losing on a trade, given that I might lose on a consecutive number of trades, so that I do not become in serious danger of being out of the game?
- Once in the trade what is the maximum percentage I am prepared to lose before exiting? Some decide this based on 'value at risk', that is a mathematical calculation based upon the probabilities of various outcomes of all open positions, and hence the value of money at risk of the positions.

Portfolio diversification

Related to good risk and money management is the issue of portfolio diversification.

'Generally, for a given level of risk you can achieve better return by diversifying. To put it differently, you have to take a greater risk for the same level of expected return if you are not diversifying. The benefit of diversification is not much more if you have 100 positions compared to ten positions. If you go from one position to ten positions, you make an enormous difference by diversifying. But going from ten to 100 there is not much additional benefit. There is an optimal level of diversification.'

While Bernard Oppetit believes in diversification, he also appreciates that it is not the rule that one should be as diversified as possible. Diversification is a method of increasing favorably the risk/reward ratio. However, being too diverse can mean you are over-stretched and cannot monitor your positions effectively. That in turn could lead to an increased risk of loss. When diversifying, remember:

- For the purposes of diversifying, there is little benefit in having individual positions which move in line with each other.
- The size of the individual positions need to be similar. Having nine positions of $100 each and the tenth one of $10,000, is not good diversification technique.
- The volatilities of the individual stocks should be similar. A $10,000, three-month sterling futures contract and a $10,000 gilts position are not comparable.

Great trading characteristics

All-consuming interest in the markets

In discussing the characteristics of great traders, Bernard Oppetit mentions first a fascination with the markets.

'One, he has to have an interest to understand what is going on in his market. That is a characteristic which very few people have. Most people feel bored. Even though they think it is exciting and they are going to have a good time, they get

> *'It takes a lot of patience and energy and motivation.'*

bored very quickly, because it takes a lot of energy to go out and dig for more – why the market is doing what it is doing, what is new, who is buying and selling, and why. It takes a lot of patience and energy and motivation to ask these questions all the time.

'The most important ingredient that is most often missing is the attitude to think hard about your market and to like it. Most people do it *en passant*, on the side or whilst thinking about other things like what they are going to do with the money.'

An interest in the market stems from your motivation for trading. Oppetit goes on to discuss motivation.

'There should be a natural drive to learn and succeed, and a drive to make money. The pressure should come from yourself, not from your boss or your client. It should not be put artificially. It should be there already. It should not be something that you force upon yourself.'

> 'Subconsciously, there are people who do not want to win.'

Oppetit has a theory about lack of adequate motivation as a cause of failure. It is a theory to which quite a few top traders subscribe.

'To a very large extent people fail because they want to fail. They want to punish themselves for one reason or another. Subconsciously, there are people who do not want to win. I do not think you can tell if you are one of those people who wants to lose. They sometimes call it bad luck, but it is often their attitude and not luck.'

Courage

The second characteristic which Oppetit considers to be of prime importance in great traders is their courage.

'It takes courage to admit you are wrong. It takes courage to face it when you have lost money and not blame it on the other guy or blame it on circumstance. It takes courage to admit that it is your mistake.'

Here Oppetit is talking about the common pitfall of traders when faced with a loss. They find it difficult to face up to the fact that they could have been wrong about a trade and consequently blame their misfortune on anything but themselves. In *The Green Hills of Africa*, Ernest Hemingway recalls how he missed an easy shot at a prize bull. He could have blamed it on his guide, who surprised the animal, but he doesn't. Instead he concludes, 'every damn thing is your own fault, if you're any good'. Great traders are responsible to themselves. A further aspect of trading requiring courage is being comfortable in the minority.

'It also takes courage to have a view that is very different from the rest of the crowd. But it is not always the case that in being a contrarian you are going to make money. Having the opportunity to be a contrarian is very important. Sometimes it puts you at the turning points and the best trades. The best opportunities are definitely very, very unpopular. Others may think you are stupid, but you have to be confident in yourself to say, "no, this is what I want to do, I believe in it". I learnt a lot when I reached a conclusion which was very unpopular and contrary to the conventional wisdom. I knew it was right and I took it, and I made money. That gives you confidence in yourself and teaches you that you are going to see things that other people do not see.'

Many traders have a problem with this type of courage. They doubt themselves whenever their favorite newsletter expresses a contrary view to their own. They may read a newspaper article and suddenly shun all the research they did themselves. Perhaps the words of William James, the philosopher (1842–1910), can offer courage. He wrote in *Pragmatism*, 'First, you know, a new theory is attacked as absurd, then it is admitted to be true, but obvious and insignificant; finally it is seen to be so important that its adversaries claim that they themselves discovered it'.

Good traders have to have confidence in their own abilities. They have to have spent hours developing a trading system and researching trades, so that once they execute them, they remain focused on the reasons for placing the trade. If they then close the position prematurely upon hearing a rumor, they might as well not have done any research or developed a system. They might as well have a system to follow rumors.

Many traders subconsciously latch on to newspaper comments in order to determine what to do with their positions, because that removes responsibility for their actions. Any losses become the

'The best opportunities are definitely very, very unpopular.'

newspaper's fault. Any profits were of course due to their own skill! Following the views of others in precedence to your own is often just another way to avoid responsibility for your actions and their consequences. It can also often be tied to low self-esteem, especially after a series of losses. Your first step to resolve this problem has to be to accept that trading success and failure is entirely up to you and you alone. You must develop a system in which you are confident. You will be confident in a system only if after testing it, you see that it works. If it does not work, improve it or discard it.

Bernard Oppetit goes on to explain a further type of courage needed in trading, hopefully only rarely.

'It takes courage to place big bets sometimes, because it can be a turning point and you know that if you miss this one things could be different. But sometimes the opportunity exists and you have to make a big bet. But it takes courage.'

An open mind

'An open mind is everything', says Oppetit. This is the third characteristic that is a key element of successful trading. He provides an example of such a mind.

'In the days after the 1987 crash I was trading OEX options in New York. Instead of taking a straight bet on direction I looked for arbitrage between strikes. For example, the November and December options were at nearly the same price. I was surprised to find a lot of them to do. Everyone who was still solvent and not 100 per cent busy meeting margin calls, was focused on direction of the market or volatility, but arbitrage is not what people did. That is open-mindedness I suppose. I did not follow the crowd in this particular case. That would probably not be as easy today because there are so many more computers today.'

This type of arbitrage opportunity exists where prices of options of different strikes are bound to increase, for example because the prices are presently the same and so have to become wider because the products are not the same.

'You can cultivate an open mind by studying a history of the markets, or even history in general. Look at things which become less relevant and how new things become more relevant.'

Few would list the study of history as an important part of trading success. But when we think about it, it makes perfect sense. Oppetit exemplifies the vastly different level on which the great traders operate. I include some books on the history of trading in the Recommended Reading section at the end of this book. Other books which I encountered while at university that you may find useful concern corporate economic history, relating in particular to the nineteenth century. Many such books deal with the early stages of the key industries of today, such as chemicals. They are often a fascinating account of how and why some industries, some regions and some countries succeeded and others failed. They give an insight into factors which cause change and how that change operates.

Stopping yourself out of trouble

As with even the most novice of traders, Bernard Oppetit will plan 'what-if' scenarios, that is, what he will do if one thing happens, and what he will do if another thing happens. Part of this planning involves the judicious use of stop-losses.

'Before entering a trade I will decide what to do if one thing happens and what to do if another thing happens. Sometimes that will involve setting stop-losses that are mental – I would never place a stop-loss for real. I know the best game in town is trying to hurt the stops. I also plan in terms of a target, but not always.'

What Bernard Oppetit is talking about here is that the floor traders can make easy money by 'taking out' stops. Everyone knows the public places stop-orders at the most obvious places – round numbers, such as 10. Imagine a stock is trading at 11–13, that is, it is 11 bid and 13 offer. A market maker would buy at 11 and sell at 13. Conversely, a member of the public is willing to sell at 11 and buy at 13. Assume a member of the public has a stop-loss at 10 bid. A market maker is likely to figure out there is going to be a stop at that price. The market maker will therefore force the price down to 10–13, buy from the stop-loss for 10 and then immediately offer it at 13. This is why Bernard Oppetit avoids stops.

'In some markets having stop-losses is a very good rule I am sure, if it is a liquid market. Once in a while you will be hurt because of whipsaw. The number one rule is "do not kid yourself". Keep an open mind. Being able to change your mind is very important. Do not allow accumulated profits or losses color your judgment. Being able to recognize you have made a mistake is very important also. Stops are useful because they enforce a discipline.'

In other words, what Oppetit is saying is that if you do not have an actual stop, it is for you to enforce the discipline of the stop. It is up to you to analyze honestly whether you should exit the trade.

TRADING TACTICS

- Gain an insight into corporate events by following the activities of key players.

- Who and what is likely to affect the share price? How and why?

- You ought to vary the *type* of analysis you do according to the time-frame and underlying security.

- Ask yourself what other market participants are thinking.

- The Swiss method: view a trade without emotion – be objective and neutral.

- Losses: Each day starts with a clean slate.

- Losses: Be honest with yourself, otherwise checks can be made payable to Monsieur Bernard Oppetit!

- Losses: Would you have opened the position today?

- Losses: Feel the fear, intend never to experience it again.

- Objectivity does not remove the art from trading.

- You do not need to risk a lot to profit a lot.

- What is the risk and the reward?

- Set a limit to how much you will risk in any one trade.

- Set a limit to how much loss a position is permitted to incur.

- Diversify, but not so much that you cannot manage all your positions.

- Great traders are responsible to themselves.

- Great traders have the courage to take a loss and admit they were wrong.

- Having the courage to be a contrarian provides excellent self-confidence when you are proved right.

- Stops can be mental instead of real.

2

Bill Lipschutz

'IT'S ALL ABOUT DOLLARS'

TRADING TOPICS

- Sources of funds and their effect on performance

- The advantages of being a 'private' trader

- Insane focus

- The Salomon trader

- Cutting back on luck

- Mentors

- Fear and anxiety

- Networking and pyramid information

- Structuring trades

Bill Lipschutz was Managing Director and Global Head of Foreign Exchange at Salomon Brothers at the end of the 1980s. If ever there was a right time and a right place for a trader, that was it – then and there. Jack Schwager, in *The New Market Wizards* (1992), described Bill Lipschutz as 'Salomon Brothers' largest and most successful currency trader'. That's not surprising when you consider that a *single* Lipschutz trade might be measured in billions of dollars, and the resulting profits in tens of millions of dollars. Schwager estimated Bill's trading alone accounted for more than half a billion dollars profit for Salomon in the eight years he was there. That's the equivalent of $250,000 profit each and every trading day for eight years.

I interviewed Bill Lipschutz twice in London. The first interview was conducted by the side of the open air roof swimming pool of the Berkeley Hotel, overlooking Green Park and Knightsbridge. The second interview took place in Surrey at the home of Mark Slater, one-time Head Currency Trader at Salomon Brothers in London. On both occasions the splendor of the surroundings meant I had to focus extra hard on my interviewee.

Working at Salomon

After earning an undergraduate degree in architectural design and completing an MBA, both from Cornell University, Bill Lipschutz joined Salomon in 1982 at the age of twenty-eight. He trained in equities and equity options and was then recruited into foreign exchange where he pioneered the development of both over-the-counter and exchange-traded currency options. The forex market is the deepest, most liquid market in the world, with daily transactions valued at over $2 trillion.

'I have to say, Salomon Brothers was certainly unique in the market place in the 1980s. It certainly was unique in foreign exchange. The way John Gutfreund [pronounced 'Goodfriend'. He gained particular notoriety from Michael Lewis's *Liar's Poker* (1990)] and Tom Strauss ran that company really gave all the traders at the firm the ability to run with the ball. Although I am sure that if I had messed up at some point in time, I would have been unceremoniously out on my butt, nevertheless that opportunity, that forum, did not really exist at very many institutions. Other firms simply didn't allow people to take positions or risks taken at Salomon. One learnt a personal responsibility and a trading maturity very quickly at the firm. No one ever said "here's your position limit, you have to cut your position".

'If someone lost a certain amount, all of a sudden their desk was empty. But it was an environment where you were always allowed to push the envelope. As long as you reached that next level successfully, you could try to push it again. That was something quite extraordinary and not something I fully appreciated at the time. In retrospect it was a really unique organization, but also with a really unique bunch of guys at the top.

'In the years I was at Salomon, performance in the company was not really measured in the same way as in asset management. The latter tends to be based on percentage return, which in itself is misleading because of additions and growth in capital. When trading a market sector for a company like Salomon there is not necessarily any actual capital dedicated to that sector. In foreign exchange most business between major market-making and trading institutions is conducted on a credit basis. There is no margin required, and therefore no dedicated capital is needed. When I was a trader at Salomon we traded out of a subsidiary which was capitalized at a million dollars. Whatever we made in a year went upstream to the parent. So, who knows what the returns were. But we had $150 billion in credit lines.'

On his own

Bill left Salomon in 1990 to form his own company, Rowayton, named after a town in southern Connecticut.

'Rowayton Capital Management started in 1991 as a vehicle to manage our own capital, which was not huge at the time. I started it with two colleagues, Bill Strack and Ron Furlong who had been at Salomon Brothers with me. We did start it with a view to ultimately managing outside capital, but we were not really sure if many of the elements of success would hold up after making the move from a big company environment to a small "on our own" environment.

'So we traded for a while, and then, at the very end of 1993, we started to raise a little outside money. My wife, Lynnelle Jones, who had been at Goldman Sachs for nine years as an institutional salesperson, not in FX but in fixed income securities, was largely responsible for the money raising. We raised about $150 million in about 18 months. That was a substantial amount coming from flat. While FX is the only thing that we traded, we developed three programs which all trade FX, but with different combinations of risk/reward objectives and different instruments. For instance, we have one product that trades no options; it is really just spot foreign exchange, mostly day trading and we don't take any overnight positions. We also have a middle kind of a product where we're using certain combinations of options. We don't do too much writing, ratio spreading or anything like that. We do a lot of intra-Europe currency spreads. Then we have a very aggressive program where we are doing a lot of "naked" writing; we are doing a lot of ratio spreads, a lot of very low delta stuff, things like that. We were able to use those programs in combination to develop other products across a broad spectrum of risk/reward objectives.

'Rowayton, as a company, closed down in late 1995, for a variety of reasons, and we currently operate a company also with an odd name, Hathersage Capital Management, which is a town in Yorkshire. Hathersage is a new company and does a number of similar things to what Rowayton did on a trading level, but we feel it is much better organized than Rowayton was on an administrative level.'

Trading with other people's money

It is often not realized that the source of trading funds can affect one's trading style and performance. As Bill Lipschutz explains, this fact is something even the most experienced traders do not appreciate until they experience it.

'I was unaware that there were these differences. Seven years ago, I had a naïve view that it does not matter whether a trader is trading Salomon Brothers' proprietary capital or trading from capital raised from ten high net worth individuals or from capital from a single source. I assumed it was all the same. The goal to my mind was to try to extract the maximum profit from the market. I didn't realize it then, but different sources will definitely imply different trading strategies. The source of capital will invariably force different trading motivations on the trader. It is not simply a question of saying, "oh, I have some capital. It doesn't matter what the source is. I will go out and do my best and at the end of the day try to make some money." It is not like that. There are many, many different strengths that come from being a corporate entity, whereas dealing for high net worth individuals you do live and die by your monthly numbers.

'The whole money-management game is a difficult game. It has not only to do with how well you perform, but what kinds of results investors are looking for in their portfolios. Absolute performance can be misleading. I can say to you, "we were up 600 per cent" over five years in our most aggressive program, and you might say, "wow 600 per cent". But that does not necessarily mean that much in and of itself, without knowing how well other currency-only managers performed and how much risk was being taken. For example, say a guy is managing $200 million, and $120 million of it is a fund that he runs with a very specific mandate. If he made 600 per cent over four years in that particular fund, he may have people pulling money out from that particular fund, because that was not the kind of variance they were expecting. The dynamics of the game are complex and often counter-intuitive.

'Look at the very different approach of George Soros, when he used to trade, and Peter Lynch. Soros was usually highly leveraged and purely and simply trying to make a lot of money. Peter Lynch, in managing the Magellan Fund, was first and foremost concerned about the preservation of capital. He was in a big bull market, he was a big stock-picker, he made a lot of money, but believe me, if the Magellan Fund is ever starting to be down at all you would have massive redemptions and you would ultimately have no fund. So the people who invest with George Soros understand they may be down 20–30 per cent in that part of their portfolio. I don't think you have any people whose whole investment portfolio is in the Quantum Fund; they are going to be diversified. The motivation of the investors is very different. Investors choose a style of managment they are comfortable with. Ultimately, the preferences of a trading manager's investors can influence the trader's trading style.

As Bill Lipschutz explains, one way the source of funding can affect your trading style is through the motivation of the lender and the terms on which the funds were granted. We all, as traders, seek more capital with which to trade. Sooner or later, after a degree of success, we decide to seek out new sources of funds, whether as a loan, which then does not require us to be regulated, or as an investment by the lender. Whatever the source of money, you must be aware that since it can affect your trading style it may also affect your trading performance. The worse time to have a deterioration in your trading performance is when the money is not your own. So before you seek new funds think hard about how it is likely to affect your trading.

Your own money

The source of trading capital can vary widely. The most obvious source is one's own capital. So, how does Bill Lipschutz trade with his own money?

'For money I have committed to speculation, as distinct from investment, one would say I have a very high risk tolerance. In essence, if I were to lose all the money I have for speculation, that would be okay. I certainly do not expect to lose it all, but I would be prepared for that outcome. Now, I would make other investments, owning my own home, that is one investment, owning a stock portfolio, that's a certain kind of investment. With the money I speculate with, I am expecting a much higher return, but I am also expecting a lot more volatility, a lot more variance. There is a significant risk of ruin, of losing it all.'

With his own funds, Bill Lipschutz is answerable to himself only and can trade as he sees fit. As he goes on to explain, with other people's money, the degree of freedom is much reduced.

Other people's money

'But, when you are entrusted with client money, it is a different business. The client says to you, "I know you can be a speculative trader. I am comfortable with that and I am willing to lose 20 per cent." I have spoken at length with clients, and we try to talk with our clients and really understand what they want. We want then to understand completely what we can and cannot do. If a guy looks me in the eye and says, "I can be down 20 per cent, no problem", I know he really means 5 per cent, because if you call him in three days and say "you know what, you're down 18 per cent, I just wanna know how you feel, so we can discuss what to do from here", he's going to forget he ever said he was comfortable with a 20 per cent loss.

Because they are not traders, they don't understand ahead of time how they are going to deal with a large drawdown. When you are charged with other people's money you have to help them and not let them get into something they are not emotionally ready for yet. You can't just go out there and wildly speculate with other people's money.

'It's often said that if you, as fund manager, buy IBM stock, and IBM goes down 25 per cent, nobody is going to fire you for that, because everybody owns IBM stock – it is the prudent thing to do. But if you go out and you buy a fly-by-night internet company and its stock goes up 80 per cent and then falls and the company goes bankrupt, then you are going to get fired. They'll pull the money from you and you will have trouble raising more money.

It's not just what kind of returns you can make, there are many other elements that motivate people in the investment decisions that they make. It goes right down to the trader level. Why did you not put that trade on at a bigger level because you knew it had an extremely good probability of going up? Well, because sometimes being wrong, even if there is a 5 per cent chance of that happening, is a whole lot worse than being right, even if there is a 95 per cent chance of that. It's the old "gee, if I make 25 per cent for these guys, they'll be really happy, and they'll think I am a great trader and I'll earn big fees". But you know what, if I lose 5 per cent for these guys, they're going to pull that money out and I am going to be close to being out of business.' So the leverage decision for the trader in this case is far more complex than merely contemplating the probability of the trade succeeding or failing. Usually, There is an entire set of issues that the trader must consider, in addition to determining the probability of the trade succeeding or failing solely on a profit basis.

> '**You can't just go out there and wildly speculate with other people's money.**'

Therefore, trading with other people's money becomes far more complicated than with one's own money. You have to consider both the likely outcome of the trade and the likely reaction of the investor to a positive and a negative trading outcome. The decisions you can make are restricted by the likely responses of your client. That in turn could impinge upon your trading performance. There can be slightly greater freedom and less pressure when trading for a firm, as Bill goes on to explain.

Playing with the company's capital

'When you manage money for individuals you have to focus on preservation of capital. When you are trading for a company, they are looking to make money. They also understand losses better. With a company it has a lot more to do with whether, as a corporation, they want to be in the business of foreign exchange, or not. It has a lot less to do with the individual traders' performances being a determinant. So if, for example, a company takes a $20 million dollar hit, they may decide to terminate the trader, but it is unlikely they will get out of foreign exchange. So, the market sector will almost never be to blame.'

Given all the constraints in trading with other people's money, the question arises, 'why not borrow from a bank as a secured loan which is repaid irrespective of performance?' Unfortunately, practical difficulties can often rule out this source of funds.

'First of all, if an investment bank, or some sort of corporate entity, was going to entrust the trading and speculation of their products with an individual, they would probably want that individual in-house. It is not so much that they are averse to that individual managing other people's money. The downside is so great politically to whoever oversees or okays that loan, that it's a job loser. If you give money to, say, Alpesh's company, and you drop a few million, then the first thing everyone is going to say is "who the hell gave that guy that money". And the next thing you know, you are fired. Whereas, if they give the money to a department in their company, then the company has made a decision, year after year, as to the business they want to be in. And if they lose money, year after year, they are not going to lose their job for that decision.'

Ultimately, one has to consider the various sources of funds available and the disbenefits of each, and weigh this up with having more capital with which to trade. Is it worth it if you have to pay for your borrowed funds with the hen that lays the golden eggs? In other words, what is the point of having extra funds if you cannot trade profitably with them?

So, before taking on new funds, ask yourself the following questions:

1. What does the lender say he or she expects?
2. What does he or she *really* expect?
3. Have I traded successfully in the past in the manner required by the lender's expectations?
4. Can I deliver what the lender *really* expects?
5. What are the consequences for me if I fail to deliver?
6. How much control does the lender want?
7. How frequently is the lender going to inquire about the performance?
8. What type of personality has the lender? Is he or she likely to pester and aggravate?
9. Can some ground rules be set?

The advantages of not being a trading Goliath

Most traders of course do not work for the leading investment banks. Most traders are private individuals who toil in whatever spare time they have to make a few accurate trades. These 'Davids', compared to the investment bank 'Goliaths', lack the same infrastructure, the support staff, the research capabilities, the state-of-the-art information and analysis software and hardware, and they lack the benefits of being surrounded by highly experienced colleagues. But the Davids do have a few advantages over the Goliaths. To trade successfully and defeat Goliath at effectively his own game, these few advantages must be 'driven home' and capitalized upon.

Advantage 1: The ability to sit on your hands

Uncomfortable, yet profitable. That is the consequence of sitting on your hands. As Bill explains, the private trader has definite benefits over his full-time investment bank counterpart in not having someone looking over his shoulder.

'When you work for a big company you don't see many traders saying, "oh man, I don't really have a good idea about the market, gee I'll read the newspapers today", because your boss is walking by, saying, "How come you're not trading?" The fact of the matter is, if most traders would learn how to sit on their hands 50 per cent of the time, they would make a lot more money.

'Let's say you take one position each day over a period of 250 trading days in a year. You know what it's going to come down to? It's going to come down to five trades, three of which are going to be horribly wrong and you are going to lose a fortune, two of which are going to be amazingly right and you are going to make a fortune. And in between, the other 245 times are not going to matter – you'll make a little and lose a little. They will be all those times when you should probably be sitting on your hands, and you'll be scrambling to get out even, or you are not paying attention and losing a large amount when there was a low probability of profiting on the trade to begin with. It all really comes down to a few decisions.

'You really need to understand the benefit of "being out of the market" if there is nothing to do, if there is no high probability trade. The whole game of trading is to continuously work for an edge. Continually take the high probability bets. Take those all the time, and by definition you will come out ahead, as long as your risk of ruin is low enough so that you do not get blown out with any one or two or three bad bets, a bad streak. So if you have someone at a big company looking over your shoulder and saying, "how come you're reading the paper, shouldn't you have a position?" the real answer is "no". But most trading management is not too much into that.'

> '**If most traders would learn how to sit on their hands 50 per cent of the time, they would make a lot more money.'**

Advantage 2: Decision-making control

On your own, with your own funds, you are the 'trigger man'. It all depends on you and you alone. Similarly, if you do not work on the trading floor, but instead have individual investors, you could have some freedom.

'Individual investors are not going to call you every day, because they don't really want to know what your positions are, whether you are long, short or out of the market. Now you, Alpesh, you are the sole decision-maker at every level: what to commit, when to commit, if to commit. I am smiling because just like you I was in university for a long time, I traded on my own – you, me, probably every other trader you are going to interview – we were all up 480 per cent at some point and the funny thing is, of course, you are looking at a universe of all successful people. If you weren't up 480, or 200 or 80 per cent or whatever it was when you were on your own, you would never have made it.'

The point Bill is making is that you ought to be having exceptional returns, probably better than your professional colleague at a bank, if you are in total trading control. If you can't do it on your own, it's unlikely to be better when you have someone looking over your shoulder. This is a point with which Kaveh Alamouti, Head of Derivatives and Arbitrage at Tokai Bank, also agreed when I spoke to him about the sizable returns my trading was producing, compared to some of the 'star' traders in investment banks. I reflected that unfortunately the stars had a 'little bit' more capital at their disposal than I!

Advantage 3: Information is profit

The greater availability of information to the private investors than ever before has meant that, rather than being at a disadvantage to their professional colleagues, they are on almost level terms with them. So, strictly, this is neither an advantage nor a disadvantage any longer.

'In 1997 information is available instantaneously far more than any of us can absorb. No one has information first. A guy sitting in his living room in Kansas watching TV can see information as fast as a trader on a trading desk now. Ten years ago, because I was at Salomon, because I had this kind of technology, I had an edge over a lot of people. I was one of the first handful of traders in New York to have a Telerate and Reuters machine in my home. And now it's commonplace.

'I wanted it at home because I knew other traders would get into work and they would have to call colleagues in London and ask them how things had looked overnight. And it occurred to me that you were going to get a second-hand interpretation doing things that way. So when I had the Telerate at home, I could come to work and know what the markets were doing. Today, almost everyone has access to that kind of information and the edge of many traders is gone.'

Do not let information availability become a disbenefit. Although you may be able to obtain information as quickly as a professional trader, they have the resources to manage it. The information problem up until the 1990s has been one of availability, cost and promptness. In the 1990s and beyond the information problem is not really about those things, it is about information management. Do not just sit back in complacency because you have the same information at the same time as Salomon Brothers. Remember you have to manage all the information available to you, otherwise it will be under-utilized.

Advantage 4: Flexibility and agility

As most people know, big things take longer to change and adapt than small things. Those are the laws of inertia and momentum. A similar law applies in trading, to the advantage of the trading 'Davids'.

'As a 'little guy' you can very quickly re-orient what your firm is doing. Many small firms will trade many different markets. If, for example, a certain market is currently yielding certain opportunities or going through structural change, big firms are much slower to realize these opportunities. For big firms there are generally many more decisions which are not related to the issue at hand that have to do with re- orienting a department. That is the nature of big organizations.'

It is important as a trader to monitor industry-wide changes, in the same way the CEO of Coca-Cola would monitor changes in the nature of the soft-drinks market. You ought then to be better placed to change product, or market if what you are trading should prove to be unprofitable, perhaps because of regulatory or other structural changes. It is an advantage which you may only utilize but once in your trading career, but it is worth bearing in mind.

Advantage 5: The pressure to perform

Small traders with their destinies in their own hands may often have less pressure exerted on them than others. However, this is not necessarily an absolute benefit.

'As far as professional traders versus the individual traders are concerned, the individual trader, does not have the same kind of pressure of someone looking over his shoulder and saying, "you ought to do this or that". But then again there is no one to force a discipline and say, "you have to cut your losses, this is too big or this is too little". Now that is probably a bad thing. You will not have, as an individual, a superior who has a dispassionate view on your positions, who can advise. A small trader who has never worked in a big firm and learnt the discipline of the big firm has trouble with discipline. He will say, "I know this is a great trade, I am going to stay with it", whereas in a big firm you often have a dispassionate superior who will say, "It does not matter. It is too big. You have got too much of a loss. You have to be out of it."'

Consequently, if you are an individual private trader, you must ensure that you recognize what beneficial outside influences (such as an imposed trading discipline) are not being placed on you, and then ensure you impose them on yourself.

Insane focus

Have you ever wondered what drives a man who has everything? Why do the richest men in the world get up and go to work each morning? Is it greed? Is it unquenchable ambition? Is it megalomania? The answer to these questions has a great relevance to trading excellence and explains why great achievers, and great traders, become great in the first place.

'If a trader is motivated by the money, then it is the wrong reason. A truly successful trader has got to be involved and into the trading, the money is the side issue. Although I am not the first to say it, I do subscribe to it. The principal motivation is not the trappings of success. It's usually the by-product – simply stated 'the game's the thing'.

Far more important than motivation is focus. I think people, really underestimate how critical focus is to success, particularly extraordinary success. Yes, it is fun. Yes, you hear traders say "I would do this for no money. I am just so into it." When you have been around as long as I have, you find people, probably yourself included, who spend inordinate amounts of time reading about or investigating phenomena to no apparent goal except that they are so fascinated by it. We observe individuals who stay up deep into the night for days trying to work out some mathematical problem, or the like.

'That's a kind of almost insane focus you must have to achieve trading excellence. You are not thinking "if I do this I will be able to buy a Porsche, or because if I do this I am going to be famous". It is something that comes from within. It's just that quest to solve the problem. That kind of focus is extremely difficult to maintain for the years and years that comprise a trading career.'

Insane focus is very difficult to comprehend unless you have experienced it yourself. It is an intensity of concentration, such that nothing else exists or matters beyond your tunnel vision. While this type of focus comes from deep within your psychological make-up, it manifests itself as extreme hard work and is different from insight or education.

'If you meet a trader who is very, very successful, and he truly, honestly, believes it is because he is smarter and faster and more insightful and more aggressive than all of his peers, question him. One thing that is common among all successful traders – whether they are formally educated or carry PhDs, they are all insightful, and hard-working.

> *'If a trader is motivated by the money, then it is the wrong reason.'*

'Think back to school, people who did well in school were usually one of two types. They were either very hard-working, organized, efficient, did all the homework, all the problems set, re-read all the chapters many more times than any normal person would, and they did very well. Or they were people, and there were fewer of these, that were just so bright and so brilliant that maybe they didn't read all of the stuff, they just had real insight. You very seldom see very bright, insightful people who are also really hard-working, with a real work ethic. You look among the top traders – they are both. They are very smart, insightful and very hard working, and very organized. They may appear to be scatterbrained, but they are not.'

Not only does Bill Lipschutz possess insane focus, he was fortunate enough to have mentors and role models who possessed it as well.

I came to know a British gentleman by the name of Mike Simpson who ran a trading desk for a market-making bank that I did a great deal of business with, and who later worked with me at Salomon. He had been in the market for 10 or 15 years before I met him. This is a guy from whom I really learned the 'nuts and bolts' of foreign exchange. Not so much options theory, but he had been in the market for a long time and really understood how foreign exchange worked, how market-making worked, how the flows worked, what caused the market to see and focus on certain things and not on other things. We became best friends over the phone over a period of three years. We both had similar backgrounds, we were both only-children and were very much about focus and hard work. He would be in his office in Tokyo by 5am his time and he would stay in his office until 9 or 10pm and then go home and get his four hours sleep. He did this for the 10 years I knew him. Of course he had been doing that for years before I knew him.'

Brilliance, intelligence, education and the desire to make money will probably lead to success. But to be a phenomenon, talent and industry are key. If you are looking for a secret to trading success, there it is.

'You have got to be really smart and you have to be willing to work really hard. You see plenty of really bright people who don't make it as long-term successful traders because they are not willing to put in the time. You can't be driven by this desire to make money. Money is a by-product. You really have to be into the whole game of it.'

> **'You can't be driven by this desire to make money.'**

When they call you 'crazy' you know you are on the right track

Insane focus is something seen in others by the very few. It is comprehended by fewer still and ultimately possessed by the fewest of all. For this reason, many times those with the capability to achieve this level of focus are pilloried by those who do not understand it. The onlookers see success and they see an industrious individual, and yet they will refuse to make the connection between the two, for fear that there is a connection. The onlookers comfort themselves with their Freudian defence mechanism: 'I don't want that success anyway, it's not worth it, and anyway you don't really have to work hard to achieve it'.

'I think people in our own industry do not understand the importance of this type of focus. You will always get people who will look at a trader and think, "God, he's up at 5.30am every morning, always working at the weekends. He has no life. I'm outta here. I'm taking my vacation. I'm going to Switzerland for three weeks." Now I am not saying people should not take vacations, but the thing is, the very best traders don't take a lot of time off. They don't want to.

Bill Lipschutz's comments remind me of the woman who said to the great violinist, Fritz Kreisler, 'I'd give my life to play as beautifully as you!' 'Madam', Kreisler replied, 'I have.' Bill goes on to explain the possible causes of this focus and drive.

'All the people you meet for this book are going to be highly motivated. Sometimes it's for deep-seated reasons: they may come from a lower economic background and there is an internal struggle, sometimes people come from situations where their fathers were highly successful and that is a psychological motivator. Ultimately, it is whatever drives an individual. Motivation is very difficult to put your finger on. The upshot of all that is the focus, that looks really odd to everyone else. People think, "what is it with that guy? He's always working. He's always doing this or that."

'I think that one thing that helped me a lot in my career was that I never stopped thinking about the market that I was involved in, about how it worked, and trying to figure out where exchange rates were going. It was not a question of saying, "gosh I am giving up time out with my friends, or I am giving up weekends here, or I am giving up sleep". I didn't think of it that way. I just wanted to trade.

The price of phenomenal success is not one many are prepared to pay. For others, a lack of talent means they do not have the currency with which to pay the price in any event. For those with insane focus, there is virtually no price to pay – they love what they are doing.

De-focus: there is more to life than trading

Of course even the most focused tend to be healthy, normal individuals. As such they do realize that their focus ought at times to be shifted to other things, such as their families. At that point, good trading requires good time and life management skills.

Inevitably you become more de-focused because other things become more important in an individual's life. You get married, have a family, where children become important to you, and you want to spend time with them. So you are not focused on the game of beating the market and your focus changes: "It's Saturday afternoon, I really ought to think about putting in those shrubs around the house or play catch with Bill, Jr." Those are the kinds of things you do instead of sitting down when the market's closed and thinking about a problem that you know you won't have a chance to think about on Monday morning.

'When you're hiring young people right out of school, they may be eager but may not necessarily have the ability to focus. That is the period in a person's life when a lot of other things are going on, for instance if they're single then they have got all that dating thing to worry about, or if they're married and maybe just having some kids then they've got that whole thing to worry about. I am not saying that you don't hire single people or people with kids; I am saying that you're looking for mature individuals who have the ability to focus on their job and handle all the other things that are going on in their lives.

'One of the things about trading is that you have got to have the ability to prioritize information extremely quickly. What's important, what's going to affect the market the bottom-line way? You have to be very, very organ- ized and prioritize so many bits of your life, to enable you to focus. Only by properly organizing his time, can a trader find those periods of time to de-focus – time taken to recharge the batteries. This combination of having the insight and a work ethic, I don't think it is intelligence particularly, it's a kind of brilliance. It is a very rare combination. I think you see it in all the successful traders.'

Child-like fascination

Much of the insane focus Bill Lipschutz discusses comes from a child-like fascination with the markets. It is having the inquiring mind, seeking to probe, prod and poke at the mysterious 'toy' that is the markets.

'The money game, or the Wall Street or City game attracts a lot of young people who are very aggressive, who want a big house and a fancy car, expensive suits, and that's fine. I would not say that that is a bad motivation or a motivation that does not exist, but as a principal motivation to success in trading I don't think it works. I think that the most important thing is the almost child-like fascination with the way the game of trading unfolds both against your fellow traders and against this unfathomable market-place, with all the nuances, all the changes – an amoebae-like amorphous thing.

'Most of the top traders have a child-like fascination with the game. Whether it's the psychological elements of the game, the technical elements of the game, whether it's the nameless, faceless aspect of a market, or them as single individuals against the market, or beating their brains against everyone else's. Long-term traders have a depth of fascination with the most arcane things. For example, talk to top fixed-income traders. They will understand and muse upon nuances of delivery details or requirements that would not even occur to you.'

It is this child-like fascination with the markets that can often lead to unforeseen beneficial side-effects, as Bill goes on to explain.

'When I was involved in trading currency options in Philadelphia, I understood the settlement, notification and delivery method so well. For example, in those days there was no automatic exercise of options. You had to notify the OCC [Options Clearing Corporation] by 5 pm on the Friday evening prior to expiration. Virtually all of those trading PHLX currency options took the Friday cut off as an absolute. However since options contracts did not legally expire until noon Saturday, exceptions could be made, which actually allowed dealers to have a window of opportunity to 10am Saturday. Well, to the extent that there might be a news item that came out in foreign exchange on Friday evening or Saturday morning, that was an advantage. Likewise, you would normally notify through your clearer on Monday morning as to what you were exercised or assigned on. But in fact the OCC made it available at 1pm on Sunday afternoon after it was allocated by lottery. So I used to go down on Sunday afternoon, once a month, because they only had delivery once a month, down to the OCC and get our runs out. I would therefore have knowledge of my positions with certainty 20 hours before anyone else knew their positions and before Tokyo opened up. I simply don't think anyone else had taken the time or had the interest to discover this information.

'So you will find an absolutely intense child-like fascination with every detail of what they are doing. They can't know more about it. It is an end in itself. They don't do it because they think, "this will make me a better trader". They want to know more because they just can't help themselves.'

The Salomon's trader: self-confident egotist?

When Bill Lipschutz worked for Salomon they were *the* investment bank. Virtually every financial superlative had been used to describe that bank in the latter half of the 1980s. It bred great traders. One of the key traits Salomon sought in its traders was an ego to withstand losses and the courage to overcome the ego and admit being wrong.

'The other big thing is that you have to find individuals who have a curious blend of ego. You clearly need to have people who have a very strong self-confidence, who have a very strong ego. In some cases you'll find individuals who manifest that as a kind of arrogance which can rub people up the wrong way at times. Sometimes that arrogance can be very important because, after all, you are going to be a loser more often than you're right. The whole idea about trading is that if you are waiting to be right 80 per cent of the time, you will never make it as a trader. You will be lucky if you are right 20 per cent of the time. You have got to figure out how to make money by

> *'If you are waiting to be right 80 per cent of the time, you will never make it as a trader.'*

being right 20 per cent of the time. It is the old 20/80 thing. [i.e. the theory that in most endeavors it is 20 per cent effort that produces 80 per cent of the results and 80 per cent of the effort that produces the remaining 20 per cent of the results]. And if you have to have that arrogance or courage, then that's alright.'

'However, it is not courageous to say, "I am going to make this one big bet even though everyone else says I am wrong". That is the home-run scenario and that is not what we are talking about. We are talking about the courage and self-confidence and ego not just to go against the crowd but to be wrong, a lot. You will find a lot of young people who cannot accept being wrong.

'It is always easier to look at a market with no positions and a clean slate and work out where it is going to go. The most difficult thing is when you have a bet on and it's the wrong bet. First of all you have to get yourself to admit it is the wrong bet and end it. That is a big psychological leap for everybody. I mean some can

> *'It is always easier to look at a market with no positions and a clean slate and work out where it is going to go.'*

do it very easily, but they have to get to that point. So, not only do you have to say "I was wrong", but then you have to go the other way. That is very difficult, so courage is very, very important.'

So, there are no absolute traits, each is counterbalanced by another complementary characteristic. For instance, the ego to overcome losses with confidence is tempered by self-analysis.

'Self-analysis and self re-evaluation has to be part of that big ego. You have to find people who are very strong emotionally and have stamina. All these things are, of course, interrelated. The ability to focus is largely rooted in stamina. You just have to have a lot of stamina.

Home-grown

As part of a Salomon's team, those hired by Bill had to have the potential to work in a team and possess all the traits needed for that. Of course leading traders are cultivated as well as born.

'At Salomon Brothers most of the people we were hiring were at that time what we called "home-grown". So you are really taking young people right out of university usually with at least an MBA and they were going to develop over a number of years. I think in a lot of ways in the industry now that has become a luxury. Now it's much more common, and also I believe at Salomon, to hire people away from other institutions who have had some degree of success.

'I think that is unfortunate. The loyalty that a person, and ultimately a group of people that work very closely together, develop for an institution and for each other is a very important part of the dynamic. Obviously trading is stressful; we are all human beings. To have colleagues who you can absolutely depend on, not only to watch a position, but for ideas, for enthusiasm, for energy, is very important. So this ability to have a solid team is greatly enhanced if a group of people are not always worried about the next biggest deal down the road.

'What I always used to look for were all the academic things that are a baseline minimum of course. You are always looking for someone who is bright, quick, sharp, and trained in certain mathematical disciplines. But that is a given. But it was always the balance between an individual's intensity and willingness to be accepting of a like level of intensity in each and everyone of his or her colleagues that formed the basis of a hiring decision. Ultimately, in large firms, the ability to work as part of a team and respect the integrity of that team, no matter how outsized an individual's contribution might be, will be the determinant of an individual's success.

A believer in luck

What is and is not luck?

Bill Lipschutz believes luck has an important role to play in trading. Luck is generally understood to be that cause which leads to a favorable outcome that was outside the control of the individual who benefited. Imagine a pedestrian crossing a busy road. He has no control over the cars on the road. He may or may not get hit. If he crosses the road with his eyes closed, he extends the sphere in which luck has to operate in order to ensure a safe passage. With his eyes closed, he would need even more luck than with his eyes open to avoid being hit. By keeping his eyes open when crossing the road he has more control over the activity he is undertaking and needs less luck to accomplish the task of crossing the road successfully. By keeping his eyes open when crossing the road the pedestrian does not ensure *for certain* that he will not be hit, but he does stack the probabilities in his favor. Stacking the probabilities in your favor is the same as reducing the sphere in which luck has to operate and is achieved by exerting as much control over events that you can control.

Since an essential part of luck is a lack of control, Bill Lipschutz tries to control as much as possible – in other words he stacks the probabilities in his favor.

'I happen to believe that a very large component of trading success is luck. Now that is not something you want to state prominently in a marketing brochure. If you did, an investor is likely to respond "well hang on, here is a guy who is telling me that it's all luck". That's not what I mean. It's not the "rolling the dice" type of luck. People who are successful traders are not gamblers. The key to being a successful trader is continuing to stack the probabilities in your favor. The more successful and the more consistent you can be in stacking those probabilities, the more you will have long-term success. There are many intangibles which a trader cannot control. What he can control is his ability to make an intelligent analysis and to place intelligent bets. By intelligent, I mean skewing the odds of a profitable outcome.

Clearly, a part of luck is putting yourself in a position where you can be lucky. You have to put yourself in a situation where you are the kind of person who seeks out the advice of others. You have to be the kind of person who is more willing to be flexible, to sit down and try to

> **'Always look to stack the odds.'**

understand new ideas. Then you are going to put yourself in a position, more often than not, where you are going to be lucky. That is another version of "always look to stack the odds".

So, by luck Bill Lipschutz means that first you ensure the odds are in your favor – you try to arrange things over which you have influence so the element of luck is reduced. Secondly, since you cannot entirely eradicate the operation of luck, you are lucky or unlucky depending on whether the outcome indicated by the probabilities actually occurs. For instance, you may bet that on a dice roll either 1, 2, 3, 4 or 5 will show. Probability theory says you should win the bet. However, as Bill explains, it will be down to luck whether or not a 6 comes up.

Realizing you are being lucky

As well as stacking the odds in your favor so that you are more likely to have a favorable outcome, you have to realize when your 'luck is in', in order to capitalize upon it.

'So as a loose analogy, sometimes you are going to be involved in trades that are going to be dead right – you are going to make your money. But you are not going to realize that it could have been a much bigger thing than you initially thought and you will get out too early. Then you are going to miss the bulk of the move. "Let your profits run and cut your losses short" is all about maximizing those few winners that you have. A trader cannot 'know' how a trade will turn out. Usually there is an element of luck involved in either staying with a position that ultimately proves to be a hugely profitable trade or in exiting very early from one that ultimately becomes a loser'.

Therefore, while it may be difficult to know whether or not your luck is 'in', you can maximize your opportunities by ensuring the probabilities are stacked in your favor.

Other aspects of luck

To be lucky as a trader not only involves luck in trading outcomes, but also other aspects of the trading environment as well, as Bill explains.

'There are so many other elements to luck. You have to be at the right place at the right time. For instance, if you are in a company, the way the company politics work enables you to take advantage of opportunities.

'If you join a trading firm, who knows where you will end up? You may end up trading junk-bonds in the late 1980s, that is an area that is hot, or you may end up in a dead-end area like Muni bonds in the late 1980s – that's luck. You may know people in the industry who teach you things which may have taken years to discover, and you can see further on their shoulders. That too is luck. So I think luck is always an important variable in a trader's career equation.'

Fear and anxiety

Great traders must not let self-confidence make them numb to a loss. They need to feel the pain of a loss yet not let anxiety become fear.

A professional athlete before a top game more often than not will say, "If you're not nervous there is something wrong". One has to have self-doubts. Maybe some are less likely than others to admit them to others or to themselves. Others are more self-reflective. Most traders are highly self-reflective. They are continually revaluating their own performance, their approach to the game. This process is indicative of a sensibility common to the best traders - it reflects both a never-ending search for improvement and an ever-present fear of failure.

'No matter how much success you have had and no matter how good you are, you have butterflies in your stomach before the big game. It is the same with the trader. You have to learn to separate fear from healthy anxiety. You certainly can't trade with fear. You can't fear to pull the trigger.

'When you go through a losing streak all the self-doubts come out and you do get very reluctant to pull the trigger. There is nothing you can do that is right. Just every single thing you do is wrong. That is something you just have to learn to control. You really have to learn how to control that fear. You have to feel the pain of a bad trade, or a wrong trade. If you don't, and are numb to it, then it's over. So you have to know what it's like to feel pain, but you can't be afraid of it.'

At some point every trader slips from having healthy anxiety to unhealthy fear. How you overcome that and return to normal trading is very much a personal thing. It is a matter of character.

'With the fear thing, overcoming that was more a personal thing because I did not know how others were dealing with it. I think a lot of that comes from inside, whatever that combination of psychological factors are that drive individuals. You discover whether or not you have it at three o'clock in the morning, when all the lights are out and all you have got is the blue, green Reuters screen glowing at you, and the position is getting worse and worse and there is no one to call or discuss it with, no one to tell you what to do.

'That is when you really discover whether you have it or not, whether you can conquer the fear and get through it and get to the analysis. You have to decide whether you can take it any more, or whether you *want* to take it any more. That is when you come of age. A lot of it is physical. Sometimes you just want to get sick. That is a very personal thing. The ability and willingness to look into yourself and force a basic character change is pretty rare. You reach down inside and you either come up with the goods or you don't. That does not necessarily mean you make money on the trade of course. It is the ability to deal with it.'

'You have to know what it's like to feel pain, but you can't be afraid of it.'

Bill Lipschutz's experiences in overcoming fear reminds me of the quote from the movie *Wall Street*: "A man looks into the abyss and sees nothing but darkness. That is when he discovers his character." As Heraclitus said: "Character is destiny." Sheer force of will can overcome any personal difficulty.

Networking: profiting from
<u>pyramid information</u>

As I commented above, information management has become more of a problem for the modern trader than information availability. That being so, it can be of great value to tap into material other people have read and digested and obtain a view from them, especially if they are likely to have a different perspective from your own. This kind of 'pyramid information' flow can permit coverage of a wider scope of information than one individual alone could ever hope to analyze. The benefit of pyramid information is not that it saves you work – there is no substitute to your own analysis – but rather, you can cover a wider quantity of material. Moreover, pyramid information allows you to get a 'second opinion' on your own analysis, thereby providing you with a safety net.

'One of the things that is very difficult in the market is that once you have a piece of information or once you assign a high probability to an outcome, you then have to make a determination as to how the market will react to that. That is not always so easy without other traders' input. So you develop a fairly robust network where, particularly in foreign exchange, different people in different countries will have different perspectives and you can tap into that. Talking over the phone taught me a lot about how different people would take the same news item and interpret it differently. Collectively these varying interpretations and the varying actions that these traders take – or do not take – based upon them, result in market action. It is critical to assess how a market with interpret and react to information prior to evaluating any position or potential position of your own.

'Having in-depth conversations is part of the ebb and flow of market information and market perception, market buzz and market feel. All that comes, in my opinion, from personal networking and personal touch and feel. If you talk to a guy, you can hear it in his voice whether he has got a bad position. I am a great believer in personal conversation – usually it happens on the phone. For instance, you call a guy who regularly carries big positions on the dollar and if you have seen a big move downwards in the dollar overnight, he can talk to you about anything in the world he wants to, but you can hear it in his voice whether he was long or short. You can also tell if he's still got the position or not.

'The other thing is that there are so many countries where the nuances of their economic and political systems and policies within those systems are very difficult for someone outside that system to understand. So, for example, if Kohl's government tries to push some sort of political initiative through, it is very important to understand what that is likely to mean for Germany, politically and economically in 2, 4, 6 or 12 months, if it is that big an event, and how that may impact the currency. By speaking regularly with a knowledgeable contact in Germany, you may be better able to assess that impact and to assess it more rapidly, than the overall market.'

Networking: what's on the market's mind?

'Another useful thing is if you get the same kind of information from several people who don't talk to each other, then that's something that's on the market's mind. If several people start saying, "German Bundesbank Reserve requirements", then you may have a look at that because several independent sources have brought up the same issue. Usually, where there is smoke there is fire.'

Of course not everyone has the privilege of being able to develop a network through the Salomon name. But even if you work alone from home, you can develop a network through the internet, and through different trading newspapers and magazines.

However, be cautious not to fall into the trap of following every-one else's analysis over your own. You have to evaluate their analysis, not just automatically fall subject to it. You cannot allow someone else's analysis to replace your own. Remember too that the analysis you receive from others is 'secondary' or 'hearsay' and there-fore has to be treated with care, caution and less weight than your own analysis from a more primary source. If you are not confident in your abilities to make proper evaluations of such information, then stay well clear.

Using analysis that you will not be using

'I have always been a discretionary trader with my analysis based on fundamentals. I am really looking to see what kind of macro-economic and political events could take place, are taking place and have taken place that could impact the currency. Now I am not a technical analyst or chartist. I don't believe in it. I don't want to take anything away from them. Some of them apparently are highly successful so they must have figured something out. Whatever kind of a trader you are, you have to be aware of perceptions in the market place, that can influence the participants' behavior. If a lot of people are charting and they think that a certain level is a key level for whatever reason – lunar, astrological, who the hell knows – then you have to be aware of it. Because it is going to cause a certain number of market participants to react and you have to be aware of it. You have to understand how that is going to affect your position. So there really is no such thing as saying that this is smart, this dumb, this is the right way or this is the wrong way. Markets move when a certain number of market participants have a certain perception. So to that extent I try to be aware of technical levels and try to factor that in.'

Therefore Bill Lipschutz's message is that whatever your views on technical analysis, you ought at least to be aware of it, because the bottom-line is all about making dollars. As General Patton said: 'I have studied the enemy all my life. I have read the memoirs of his generals and his leaders. I have even read his philosophers and listened to his music. I have studied in detail the account of every damned one of his battles. I know exactly how he will react under any given set of circumstances. And he hasn't the slightest idea of when I'm going to whip the hell out of him.'

'There is only one basic trading rule that everything feeds back to, that is, "it's all about dollars". You can think you're right, but if you didn't make any money then, guess what, you were wrong. Again it goes back to "dumb dollar, smart dollar". You could be the biggest idiot in the world but if at the end of the trade there are dollars in the bottom-line, then you were brilliant.'

Although Bill Lipschutz does not use technical analysis, it nevertheless has its uses for him. First, it gives him an indication of what other market participants are thinking. Secondly, it can be useful in determining market entry and exit.

'You will be aware that some traders use technical analysis as a kind of an overlay to look at entry and exit points. The problem with fundamental analysis is that it is very broad based and it is very difficult to sharpen your pencil and say, "do I buy it here or there". You have to be aware of all these technical techniques, such as momentum, because a lot of market participants use them and so they can affect the market.'

Structuring trades

Encapsulating the idea

After traders have formed a view on likely future price changes they have to encapsulate that idea into a trade. The simplest form of trade would be to buy the underlying asset where the expectation is of a price rise. However, depending on one's view, more complicated strategies can give rise to more optimal results.

> *'You could have the dead right idea and lose money.'*

'The next step is structuring the trade. There are a million ways to structure the trade and the devil is in the detail. You could have the dead right idea and lose money. If your timing is slightly off, you could lose. You have to structure your trade in a manner that increases your probability, your upside, and decreases your downside. And that is all the game really is, a constant series of these kinds of trading decisions.'

'For example, there are a lot of ways to be long the yen. You can buy the yen, buy calls or sell puts. If you want to be long the yen and yen volatility is very low, then buying calls is going to be very attractive. If volatility is very high, then maybe selling puts is very attractive. But if the volatility is extremely high, then selling puts may not be the best thing – maybe just buying the underlying asset may be the best thing. So the manner in which you express the trade idea should be with an eye to getting the other elements of the trade on your side, stacking the odds in your favor.

'For example, if you are buying an out-of-the-money call spread and the leg of the spread that you buy is say, 2 per cent out-of-the-money and the leg of the spread that you sell is 5 per cent out-of-the-money, then if you turn out to be right about the trade and the leg that you bought is now at-the-money, then the volatilities will change relative to at-the-moneys. In other words, when you first buy that spread, both legs will be trading higher implied volatilities than at-the-money. But one leg becomes at-the-money, and you realize you have lost some money because the at-the-money will now trade at at-the-money volatility. So that too is a dynamic to be aware of, especially if you go into ratio spreads, because if you are right on direction you may want to buy one of the legs back and that short leg is likely to hold its value.'

However, remember that it does not follow that the more complex the trade, the more money you will make.

'Gil Leiendecker, my boss for many years at Salomon Brothers, used to say, there is smart money and dumb money. But at the end of the day a dollar is a dollar is a dollar. What he is trying to say is it doesn't really matter how you make the money. A lot of young traders, for example, lose money in, say, IBM. They then want to go back into IBM and make their money in that stock. That's irrelevant. You don't have to force yourself to trade in IBM just because you lost it in IBM. The market has no idea. The bank account doesn't know where the dollar came from. Gil used to say to me, "couldn't we just buy or sell the dollar and take our profit. Why do we have to do options and all these complicated things." What he meant was, "smart money, dumb money". Sometimes you can   step back and say "buy it" and if it goes back you can say "sell it, thank you".'

> **'There is smart money and dumb money. But at the end of the day a dollar is a dollar is a dollar.'**

Evaluating the upsides and downsides

Structuring a trade to capture the upside also involves ensuring there are downside protections.

'Of course when you first put on a trade you do have target levels, levels at which you think you are wrong. The price levels of those targets should be determined as a result of your trade idea analysis. The size should be determined as a result of your absolute dollar loss constraints. For example, let's assume that the current price level of dollar yen is 125 yen per dollar. Let's further assume that your analysis of the latest round of trade negotiations between Japan and the United States leads you to believe that the yen may weaken to 130, but due to technical considerations should not strengthen beyond 122.50. Further analysis of the pricing of yen options leads you to determine that the optimal trade structure will be to simply sell the yen against the dollar in the spot market. How large should the position be? The answer lies in the asset size of the account you are doing the trade for and its loss limit. If you are only prepared to take a three percent loss on a ten million dollar account, then it follows that you should buy $15,000,000 against the yen. If you are wrong on the trade, you loss will be $300,000 and if your anaylsis was correct and you sell the position at 130, your profit with be £600,000.'

'This looks quite simple, but the above description is a static analysis in a highly dynamic situation. There is always new information coming in. You must continually re-evaluate your position in the light of the new information – including any new price level itself – and adjust your target levels accordingly. Of course that can be very dangerous in terms of when you think you are right and it keeps on going against you and you keep adjusting downwards. But that is not what I am talking about. You have to correctly interpret the new information. Above all you must not lose sight of your absolute dollar constraints.

Therefore the use of targets and their re-evaluation in the light of new information is a key aspect of trade structure. One way to protect yourself against the downside is to ensure there is a multiple upside to downside.

'With a trade you always look at a multiple upside to downside. But how much greater? A good rule of thumb for a short-term trade – 48 hour or less – is a ratio of three to one. For the longer-term trades, especially when multiple leg option structures are involved and some capital may have to be employed, I look for a profit to loss ratio of at least five to one.'

Options are sometimes used by traders as insurance against an adverse move. For example, if particular traders are expecting an upward move in prices, they may buy calls. However, to protect themselves against an adverse downward move they may also buy some puts or sell different strike or series calls.

> *'Just know what you are prepared to lose.'*

'I have always felt that using options as an insurance policy is probably not appropriate for the professional trader. It may be appropriate in market sectors where there is not much liquidity or if price movements are often discontinuous. However, as neither is the case in foreign exchange, a professional trader who is 'close to the market' at all times that he is carrying an open position will be able to cut the position and get out if it goes against him. Only in the infrequent case of a professional who carries extremely large positions which alter these price characteristics of the market would I favour the use of options as insurance.'

As well as downside protection in any particular trade one also needs downside protection against a losing run.

'I think risk is asymmetrical. To achieve successful longevity, you have to focus on your losses, or drawdowns, or whatever you call them. It's very simple. Just know what you are prepared to lose. It doesn't matter how big, little, right or wrong your position is. You have to know what you are prepared to lose. I don't mean mentally prepared; I mean mathematically what can be lost when you enter a trade. You must not put yourself out of business. You have to be back. You have to be there tomorrow, the next day and the day after. If you manage the downside, the upside will take care of itself.'

All this focus on the downside begs the question 'when does one close a position?'

'There are two reasons for closing a position, I think. One is if the scenario, or a variation of the scenario that you were expecting to occur, clearly was not going to occur. An easy example would be if you expected a certain policy if this person from the left wing of the political spectrum were to win the close-run election, and he does not win. The second reason is, correct scenario or not, you have reached your pre-trade drawdown limit. End of discussion; you must exit the position.'

Mentors: the Salomon experience

There is more to what makes a great trading mind than merely how it takes losses and handles risk and profits. There are a fascinating and unique set of experiences which mold that mind in the first place. Bill related a couple of those formative and informative experiences.

'In my case, there were some early influences on me in my professional career. Several senior people who had been in the markets took me under their wings and taught me a lot. My first boss at Salomon's, Gil Leiendecker, was Global Head of Foreign Exchange for about seven years before myself. He had a way about him. His background was not foreign exchange, but in fixed income, but it was always Gil's personal code of conduct and leadership ability which distinguished him from others.

'I learnt mostly about integrity in the markets from him. How you act and how you treat your colleagues. After all, you are focused, driven, high-strung, you are tired, you are pushing your stamina to the limit. People say and do things which they regret later. Gil taught all of us in his department a lot about how one deals with adversaries in the market and colleagues in the market'.

'Gil had great phrases like, "there are a lot of gray areas in the market, especially OTC [over-the-counter, as opposed to traded on an exchange]". Grey areas in the sense that people make mistakes sometimes. Do you hold the guy to a deal? Gil would always say

'Think about whether you would want your mother to read about it in the *New York Times* tomorrow, and if the answer is no, then don't do it".

'Gil had a million of these sayings. I remember I went through a period where I became very demanding of myself and ultimately of those around me. However not everyone was as driven or as focused as I would have liked them to be. For instance, if it's a Friday night and it's this guy's anniversary and you want to be there until 10pm and you expect him to be there, then you get angry that he is not. Gil would say to me, "remember something Bill, people come in, and you can yell and you can scream, and you can expect them to give more than they're willing to give, but at the end of the day people just want to have a nice day. A nice day to you, Bill Lipschutz, means a certain thing. A nice day to a guy who's a clerk (not that that's a lesser thing) or another trader next to you means something different. You have got to figure out what is a nice day for each person." Anyway, he taught me a lot about how to interact in a human fashion with people in a marketplace. That is something that is generally overlooked today in the 'care and feeding' of young traders. That really helped me a lot in my career.

'Another fellow that I learnt a lot from, was a great senior trader who at the time was in New York with Marine Midland Bank. He was Tony Bustamonte. He would take me to lunch once a month, which was a big thing because you tended not to leave your desk during the day and because Tony was such a renowned market figure. We mostly discussed things like forwards, the emergence of options as an FX instrument and, of course, the general direction of the dollar. He was a real mentor. So in my case I was very lucky to have had a lot of mentors on a lot of different things, not just about "this is how you buy them and this is how you sell them". They were mentors on the more human aspects of how you survive in this business. For me personally that has really been part of the success.'

The quality and availability of mentors is out of your control. Therefore you have to fall back on luck. These aspects of trading success always seem to be neglected and forgotten.

'That's why luck plays such a big role. All these things coming together. It's quite amazing actually. When you meet someone who is good for you, your whole life goes down a different path and it's like a tree whose branches make contorted shapes as the tree grows. You could never pick that contorted route you are ultimately going to take. It's funny some of the things I remember – just comments that people made that they probably don't even remember.'

Most of us can probably relate to the sentiments expressed by Bill Lipschutz. There will have been individuals in our lives who have set us on different paths from those we would otherwise have taken. For myself, I recall a phrase once stated by my politics tutor, Dr Nigel Bowles, at Oxford. He told me that '90 per cent of students at Oxford, let alone less august institutions, are dull, boring, dare-nothing, take-no-risks, play-it-safe types. The majority of the remainder achieve first-class degrees.' That one comment, which he has probably forgotten ever saying to me, has remained with me for years. Like the types of statement Bill mentions, it is 'life-path altering'. And so it is with trading too that we should, if at all possible, find mentors and place ourselves in a position where our outlook and perspectives can be altered for the better and forever.

TRADING TACTICS

- How will the source of funds affect your trading?

- As a private trader make full use of your advantages: the ability to sit on your hands; decision-making autonomy; information availability; flexibility; less pressure to perform.

- Do you have insane focus – the child-like fascination with the markets – which others think is crazy?

- Ego has to be tempered with self-analysis.

- Can you withstand being wrong 80 per cent of the time and still make a profit?

- Reduce the sphere in which you need luck to operate by stacking the odds in your favor through controlling as much as you can.

- What's on the market's mind?

- Even if there are types of analysis you do not believe in, be aware that if it's popular it will affect prices.

- Trades need to be structured to optimally utilize your view of the market. Give equal thought to formulating your idea and to the structure of the trade.

- However, the trade need not be complex to be optimal.

- Trades with multiple up to downsides will ensure long-run profitability.

3

Pat Arbor

'YOU HAVE GOT TO STEP
OUT AND DO SOMETHING
AND TAKE A CHANCE
AND GET YOUR TEETH
KICKED IN.'

TRADING TOPICS

- The nature of risk and risk management
- Progressive trading
- Exiting trades
- Top trading qualities

Pat Arbor is the Chairman of the Chicago Board of Trade – the world's largest and oldest futures and options exchange – a post he has held since 1992. Prior to the Chairmanship, he served on the Board of Directors from 1990 to 1993 and as Vice Chairman from 1987 to 1990. He has been a member of CBOT since 1965. He is also Chairman of the Board of Directors of the MidAmerican Commodity Exchange, an affiliate of the CBOT. An independent trader, he is a principal in the firm of Shatkin, Arbor, Karlov & Co.

Nineteen ninety seven has seen three of his greatest achievements as Chairman, and ensured that CBOT will remain the leading securities exchange in the world well into the next millennium. First, 9 May was the date of the historic LIFFE–CBOT link which permits trading of the world's two biggest debt contracts at both exchanges. The two contracts are LIFFE's 10-Year German Government Bond (bund) futures and options contracts and CBOT's 30-Year US Treasury Bond (T-Bond) futures and options contracts.

Secondly, 5 June saw the award to CBOT by Dow Jones and Company of a license to offer trading in options on futures and in futures contracts based on the Dow Jones Industrial Average. Such contracts have been dubbed the 'last great futures contracts'.

Thirdly, the CBOT recently inaugurated its new $182 million financial trading floor, the largest trading floor in the world.

A native of Chicago, Pat Arbor started his career as a math teacher and later served as mayor of Harwood Heights, Illinois.

Arbor is active in government and community affairs, charitable organizations and banking. He was appointed in October 1994 by President Clinton to the Board of Directors of the Western New Independent States Enterprise Fund, charged with promoting private sector development in Belarus, Moldova and Ukraine, and capitalized with $150 million in foreign assistance appropriations. He also serves as a member of the Advisory Board for the United States Association for the United Nations High Commissioner for Refugees.

Arbor serves on the Executive Committee of the Board of Trustees of Loyola University of Chicago, overseeing a budget of $678 million as well as a student population of 14,000 and the largest medical center under Catholic auspices in the United States. He is a member of the Board of Regents of Chicago's Mercy Home for Boys and Girls, chairs the Home's Development Commission, and is a member of the Corporate Board of the Mission of Our Lady of Mercy. He was appointed in October 1996 by the late Joseph Cardinal Bernadin to the board of the Catholic Charities of the Archdiocese of Chicago. He was active in the successful drive to bring the 1996 Democratic National Convention to Chicago, serving as co-chairman of the finance committee of the Committee for '96, and as a leading sponsor of the event. Also, he has authored numerous articles on finance in leading professional and academic journals.

Arbor sat for 17 years on the Board of Directors of the First State Bank & Trust Company of Park Ridge, a $325 million bank holding company, which was sold to First of America Bank Corp. He also has served on the public board of London Investment Trust (LIT), PLC, a publicly held holding company in London.

The Chicago Board of Trade

The role of the Chicago Board of Trade is to provide markets for its members and customers and oversee the integrity and cultivation of those markets. The primary method of trading at the CBOT is open outcry, during which traders meet face-to-face in trading pits to buy and sell futures contracts. The secondary function of CBOT is to provide opportunities for risk management among farmers, corporations, small businesses and other market users.

The Chicago Board of Trade was formed in 1848 by 82 merchants to promote commerce in the city by providing a place where buyers and sellers could meet to exchange commodities. In 1865 the CBOT formalized grain trading by developing trading in futures contracts. Just over 110 years later, with capitalist societies having shifted away from agrarian reliance, and with a return to floating currencies and the proliferation of US government-issued debt, largely due to the Vietnam war, CBOT expanded its contract offerings to include a menu of financial futures instruments. Thereby the exchange ensured it remained at the forefront of trading innovation and a microcosm of capitalist development. More than 3600 CBOT members trade 57 different futures and options products at the CBOT, resulting, in 1996, in an annual trading volume of 222.4 million contracts.

I first met Pat Arbor at his offices at the Board of Trade. He was wearing his trading jacket and looked exhausted. We discussed the interview and I dashed off to catch my flight to London. We met again one month later in London and I interviewed the Chairman over lunch. The previous day he had flown to London from New York by Concorde, having finalized the trading licenses for the Dow Jones contracts. Again he looked exhausted. It became evident that his achievements are due in large part to his drive and energy. For a man in his 60s he could run circles around men one-third his age.

Risk: why take it?

Risk-taking is older than literature. As far back as 3500 BC, the Mahabharat, the holy scriptures of the world's oldest religion, Hinduism, describes a game of chance played with dice on which kingdoms were wagered. Little wonder then, as Peter Bernstein states in *Against the Gods* (1996), 'the modern conception of risk is rooted in the Hindu–Arabic numbering system that reached the West seven to eight hundred years ago'. Not only is risk-taking for pleasure and profit an ancient activity, it is also the basis of all economic development. Indeed, any form of development is impossible without people being willing to take risk. Without risk-takers, there would be no contracts, no goods made or bought, no services tendered. Literally, civilization would come to a halt without the willingness to take risk.

'Nobody ever achieved greatness by doing nothing. You have got to step out and do something and take a chance and get your teeth kicked in. A good trader has to engage in some acts which are considered risky. We took a risk in trying to get the Dow Jones contracts. We won and the Mercantile Exchange lost. Obviously, I am glad the way it came out. We took a risk on the LIFFE link. We had a lot of our members who resisted the link; they were very parochial, they thought everything began and ended in Chicago.

'I took a risk on our new building – $182 million of state-of-the-art 60,000 square foot trading facilities. It was something which was ignored by my predecessor as too risky and too controversial, but I believe it was instrumental in our being awarded the Dow Jones contracts. I had tremendous opposition from our membership on that too. They argued it was too much debt to take on. I think it is the same in the pit. You have to step forward and take a risk.'

Managing risk

For as long as there has been risk-taking there has been the desire to control risk, the desire to have certain precise quanta of risk. While risk is the probability of an uncertain adverse event, insurance is the benefit gained from the occurrence of that adverse event. It is because of insurance, which reduces risk to levels with which we are comfortable, that we are willing to undertake risky activities. Essentially, all the profits of risk-taking activities stem not merely from taking the risk in the first place, but from managing that risk all along with insurance, so that the risk is not so great that we refuse to undertake the endeavor. The warranties provided with goods purchased are insurance, the visual inspection of the second-hand car is insurance, the word of honor of the seller is insurance. Without insurance, there would be less risk taken, with less risk taken there would be less progress and development.

As Pat Arbor explains, great traders take risks and manage risks.

'I think great traders certainly have to have a psychological stability about themselves, but not too much stability, because one has to have a certain flair for risk. It is a fine psychological blend you have got to look for in a trader; the ability to take risk, the ability to have some courage, coupled with stability in the psychological make-up. I think the great traders have to have a greater appetite for risk than the normal person or the poorer traders. Then the question is how they manage that risk, the discipline they impose on themselves to manage that risk.

'One has to be able to manage the risk. By that I suppose I mean, I guess it ties in with discipline also, the ability to manage the trade. A great trader once told me, "it doesn't really make much difference what you do on your initial transaction, whether you buy it or sell it", and all things being equal the market can only do one of three things: go up or down, or stay the same. But the question is what you do after you make the trade, how you manage it. What I mean by that is that if you are wrong, do you have an exit strategy? If the market goes against you, what do you do? Many times traders do the wrong things.'

By risk management, Pat Arbor is talking about taking decisions to reduce the risk of further adverse events and to increase the probability of beneficial events. He provides several options.

> *'It doesn't really make much difference what you do on your initial transaction.'*

'I would say that you certainly don't formulate the strategy before, but if it starts going against you, you had better start formulating exit strategies and alternatives pretty quickly. You don't have much time very often and you have to be pretty quick. Obviously, you could balance the position against options – that's one thing. You could neutralize the position using options or futures, if you are in an options position. You can liquidate the position. But one thing you never want to do is add to a bad trade. If the trade is against you, one of the cardinal rules of trading is you should never add to it. Obviously you've been wrong. It would be much better to wait until the trade surged back and returned to the original point of entry, and then started working for you, it would be better to add to it then, than add to it if it were a loser.'

Pat Arbor manages risk by balancing it, usually through the use of spreads and hedges. A spread or hedge is the combination of at least two positions, one of which gains when the other loses. In other words, it is a risk position added to an insurance position.

'In most cases the risk is balanced. In my own trading I have always tried to be a spreader or arbitrageur. If I am long one month soybeans, then I am generally short another month soybeans. And I generally do soybeans or bond spreads. If I am long bonds, then I am short 10-year notes. Sometimes if I am long a commodity outright, then I might be long corn and short soybeans or long soybeans and short corn.'

'As much as you can you try to get it apples to apples, but much of the time it's apples to oranges. You never want it apples to elephants because there is absolutely no relationship there. So, I'll give you an example. I just had the Australian Wheat Board in. The Australian Wheat Board uses our markets tremendously. The Australian wheat is a hard red winter wheat. It is a higher quality wheat than we trade at the Chicago Board of Trade. Our wheat contract is a soft red winter wheat. It is not a very good milling wheat (it's a high-grade feed wheat), but the market has liquidity and depth. Even though the Australian Wheat Board is exporting and trying to hedge their exports out of Australia, they use our soft red winter wheat contract even though the basis is not many times the same. But it generally moves in the same direction, close enough for the hedge to work. That is a case where you have an orange and a lemon maybe. A good hedger takes the view that any port in a storm will do, you just need shelter, you need to manage that risk. So, if a ship is at sea and about to founder on the rocks, they will pull into any port – any port will do.

'It is the same thing with huge international hedgers. Even though it may not be the exact product, it comes close. We have seen that in our bond market. Mortgage dealers will use our 10-year contract although they may be looking for a 7-year maturity. They will use our 10-year contract and mix it up a little bit and come pretty close to hedging the risk in the underlying product for which they need a 7-year maturity product.

'A pure spread trader when asked at the end of the day "was the market higher or lower?" very often does not know. But if you ask him what the November–July bean spread is, he will say "158–168". He will know exactly what the ratio spreads are between corn and soybeans or bonds and 10-year notes, S&P against the NASDAQ or OEX. So a good spread trader or arbitrageur may not know or care if the market is up or down. All there has to be is volatility and movement and they will figure out a way to capture that. They will be able to figure out a way when they see things out of balance.

> '*A good hedger takes the view that any port in a storm will do.*'

'I remember once when I was trading back in the 1970s, a very large commercial grain company put an order in to buy some soybeans. On that particular day the soybean market had moved down to limit – it was limit sellers, because some bearish news had come up. More importantly, the November–January bean spread had gone from November being 34 over January to being only 17 cents over January in the pit. Now you must understand, the market had gone limit sellers but it settled in November, it went limit sellers where the settlement the previous day was. So November was offered 34 cents over where the January was offered. For example, let's say January was offered at $7 and the November was offered at $7.34 cents.

'One of the world's largest grain companies came in with an order to buy some November beans. They bought 500,000 bushels of November beans and I managed to sell them 100. I was relatively new at the time. I went over and bought a hundred January beans at $7 and sold November beans at $7.34, and went over to a spreader in the pit and asked "what is January–November?" and he said, "I will sell it to you 17 over". I did a hundred with him at 17 over and made $17,000 dollars just like that. Now the grain company bought 500 bushels, so they gave 5 × $17,000 away. That's $85,000. I went over to the desk and I told the fellow what had happened. He said, "I was told to buy November beans, and that's what I bought". I said to him, "but you could have bought January and done the spread and saved yourself $85,000". Yet they made that mistake.

'So a spreader capitalizes on those mistakes. People sometimes make mistakes, sometimes the market is out of kilter. When the Hunts were in the silver market in the 1970s, they started buying silver aggressively either at the Board of Trade or Comex, and very often those two markets would be out of line. Where the Chicago silver was higher than New York, the arbitrageurs would step in and correct that. That is why I say the market is a great determinant because it will always self-correct. There may be aberrations in the market, but the market corrects.

'As far as speculating in the silver markets, the Hunts really were undone and broken by all the mammas and the papas in the United States of America, when they saw the price of silver go up to $50 an ounce. They all went into their silverware cabinets and there was a tremendous proliferation of smelting companies in the United States;

all of a sudden the silver was being melted down and made into ingots and delivered at the exchanges.

'So these aberrations occur but they always self-correct, whether on the floor of the Board of Trade or by a speculator off the floor of the market. Seeing the Hunts get carried away with this spree, all of a sudden the supplies of silver started to build up around the country as the silverware started to be melted down. It's the same thing. You just have to take advantage of situations that are out of balance.

'I have just seen that happen with the bund contract. We are trading bunds at the Chicago Board of Trade and it has been a big success for us. We are averaging 8000 or 9000 contracts a day. I was watching everyone in the pit and they were very active and excited because the bunds on ATP were up at two or three ticks what they were bid for in Chicago. This was just momentary, so arbitrageurs started buying on ATP and selling in the futures pit in Chicago. So there are so many markets now and so many ways to balance risk.

> ### 'Your first loss is your best loss.'

'You also spread because you may not be prepared for the straight position. You may like the position, you may be bullish on the position, and it may not be going well. You would like to maintain your position, possibly moderate it a little by selling something against it. You may be long soybeans outright, and you can neutralize it a little by selling soybean meal, or soybean oil or some corn against it. Your S&P position may not be going so well and you may want to sell bonds against it. You are keeping your position but cutting your profit potential. Of course you could just take the loss. But where you may not do that and have a spread instead is where you think you are right and like the position. Then you tend to neutralize it a little bit to mitigate the loss. I don't think that it is a superior strategy. As I said before, your first loss is your best loss, and the thing to do is probably to get out straightaway.'

Spreading or hedging as a form of risk management is not necessarily suited to everyone, as Pat Arbor explains in the next section.

Finding a style to fit

'As a trader you must decide what you are. You are either a specu-lator, spreader or local scalper. You have to fit into one of those categories. Me, I am suited to spreading. To find what suits your personality you just have to see whether or not you make money at what you're doing. I have had people come into the office, saying, "I am a great trader", I say, "you're right", they say, "I know how to trade". I say again, "You're right" and they say, "I predicted that the market was going to go up or down", and I say again, "You are right. But the bottom line is whether you make any money."

'Our business is unlike any other; you may be a good writer but there is no way really to tell. Even if you make a lot of money, you may be the world's worst writer, but you may make money out of it, but not business. That is about how well you do. That is the bottom line in our business. You could be a great lawyer, and nobody would know. You might get credit, acclaim or reputation, but in our busi-ness there is a direct measurement and that is the bottom line. So I said to this fellow, "You are not a good trader because you have not made any money".'

So, while hedging can be a good way to manage risk, whether or not you wish to be a hedger depends on what trading style makes money for you given the type of trading personality you are.

From small acorns: progressive trading

Progressive trading is the name I have given to the idea that the best trading result and long-term profitability is assured through a 'slow and steady' style of trading. I have yet to meet a great trader who advocates wild risks in order to make spectacular home-runs.

'The best traders I think are those who try to make a little bit every day. You surely have your success stories – those who hit home-runs – but if you take a record or study of the home-run hitters against those who try to hit singles every day, the success rate of the former is a lot less than the latter. So a good trader ends

> 'A good trader ends up being one who accumulates capital over a period of time.'

up being one who accumulates capital over a period of time. Those people who try to make it all at once have difficulty.

'I once remember explaining this to a young Italian trader and I said to him, "It's *uno fagiolo* (one bean) a day". If you try to put one bean in a bag per day, *uno per uno*, then at the end of the month you are going to have 31 beans in the bag. But if you try to put all 31 beans through the mouth of the bag you will spill a few, and in some cases you will not get any of them in. So it is better to build it up one day at a time, in a small manner, slowly. It's tempting not to do that when you see the George Soros's and Niederhoffers, but if you live by the trading sword, you die by the trading sword.

'A great trader once told me, and I am not sure if I necessarily agree with this, but this was told to me by Lee Stern, that "in life trading or trying to amass capital, many times you lose one-third of your capital, and then you will make it back and gradually build it up, and you may lose one-third again, and then you build it back up". It is like climbing a flight of stairs, as you go up three stairs and you go one step backwards, you will get to the top of the stairway but it's going to be a slow upward movement.'

Implicit in Pat Arbor's advice about 'progressive trading' is the idea that it is all right to be out of the market.

'The discipline not to trade – that's a big one. A lot of people don't realize that. A lot of people think you should stand there all day long and be in the market all day long. There are times when the market is so dead or so illiquid that you should not be trading. There are times when the market is terribly volatile and makes no sense and you should not be trading. It is generally the former though. I have seen people stand there all day long when there is nothing going on, just a few locals in the pit. They will put a position on out of boredom. Then they can't get out of it easily. I say to them, "well, you shouldn't be trading. There's nothing going on. Take it easy. Take a walk. Go off to the coffee shop."'

Getting out of the painful trade

One of the most difficult issues which faces a trader with each and every trade is knowing when to exit. Pat Arbor has several indicators that tell him when the time is right.

'Well, the first thing obviously is that if the trade has gone against you and you are losing money on the trade, that is certainly the first red flag that goes up. The second thing is your pain tolerance, your money tolerance. If it is a small loss, you can tolerate that, but if it gets to an amount that hurts, then you know it is significant and you should be exiting the trade.

'A lot of it is measured by pain – pain to the pocket-book, pain to the wallet, pain to the psyche. But generally speaking, the trader's adage is that "your first loss is your best loss". Obviously, in the beginning the loss is not too bad, and generally speaking that is the best time to exit a trade. If you have a trade that goes against you, but not by too much, and it stays there and lingers around there for a while, you sometimes can tolerate that. But if it continues to worsen, you'll know in your gut when to exit.

'Some people have specific standards, especially big trading advisors – they have built-in stop-loss ratios as a percentage. For example, that they are not going to lose more than one to five per cent of the money they are handling.

'I was always a floor trader who reacted to this kind of a thing by gut instinct. But there are traders who impose specific monetary or percentage standards upon themselves as to how much loss they will incur, whether it is based on their net worth or the amount of trading capital they have, or the amount of money they are going to lose on a specific trade.

'The trouble with the loss is not only the loss of money but it's the ego'.

'I have seen traders in the pit, as soon as they have a loss they take them immediately, and they continue to take these losses. I remember one trader in particular who had trouble taking these losses and he had a psychological problem, and I am sure he went to see a psychiatrist or a psychologist, or a therapist or a shrink. I saw his behavior change in the pit. Every time he had a trade and it made a loss, he was very ostentatious. He was very showy, very demonstrative about taking the loss. Everybody knew what he was doing. I have seen other traders do it very quietly.

'You see, the trouble with the loss is not only the loss of money, but it's the ego. The mind games it plays with you, because we all like to think that we are smart and like to have confidence in ourselves. When something goes against us, it not only hurts our wallet, it also hurts our ego. The temptation is, if I bought something at five and now it is three, then, if I liked it at five, it must be even better at three. But the market is a great determinant, it is telling you something. 'The market has intelligence that is beyond what our minds can comprehend. We must view the market like Deep Blue, the computer that won chess games against Gary Kasparov. The market is the accumulation of all the information that there is, and the market indicates that price.

'The market is always right. No one is smarter than the market. I have seen people come down to the floor with IQs of 150, PhDs, MBAs from Harvard, and not do well, because they think they are smarter than the market. We pay and collect according to the settlement prices, the marks at the end of the day. And one has to remember that. The market is smarter than any trader. You can't really beat the market. Contrarian traders try to bet against the market and some are very successful, but most of the time it is very difficult. They try to fade the market either on the highs or the lows, and that can be very risky, although I know traders who have built mathematical models and systems which do that sort of thing.'

> '**The market has intelligence that is beyond what our minds can comprehend.**'

The message from Pat Arbor is that the market is not something that is fought, it is something that exists. One never makes the first move against the market, one reacts to the market. You are not up against the market or trying to outwit it. Consequently, with that perspective you should have less of a problem with your ego taking offense at losses.

'Wanna be a trader?'

So what advice does the Chairman of the largest securities exchange in the world have for someone who wants to be a trader?

'When I first came to the Board of Trade I didn't know much about trading, or what to do. My first trades were terrible. It took me some time to figure out who were the successful traders and who were not. Then I began to study them and to emulate them. I noticed that the spreaders, arbitrageurs were the ones who were driving the nicer cars and had the better lives, so I tried to be a spreader. Find someone who is successful and try to copy them.

'There are certain qualities you can see in a good trader: alertness, quickness with numbers. I just met David Kyte for the first time a couple of months ago. He's sharp, he's quick, he's incisive, a bit brash, gutsy – all the marks of a good trader. But there is a certain discipline about him too, a certain swagger, "machoness". You look in traders for an ability to do many things at the same time. You have to be able to talk to one person and listen to another and look at a third. You have to be multi-dimensional; and then take all that and focus it on what you are trying to do.

'We notice, certainly in floor traders, certain athletic abilities. Most good traders have good athletic ability. Some don't, Richard Dennis for instance. But even he, who is a good friend of mine, plays tennis. There has to be a good competitive instinct in you, and   dexterity, hand–eye–mind co-ordination. There has to be some competitive juices flowing. At our firm we have had football players, basketball players, runners. The athlete that does the best on the floor seems to be the tennis player. Perhaps it is the hand–eye–mind co-ordination and the discipline.

'Trading off-the-floor is very different from trading on the floor. Trading off-the-floor requires a lot more patience, a lot more information, a longer view of the trade, because it is very difficult to make a lot of small quick profits. It requires a lot more discipline. It's generally easier on the floor if you can stand the physical aspects.

'When I started there was not much competition – you started on the floor, found someone successful and copied them. Nowadays it's all changed, the big money is being made by the off-the-floor traders, the proprietary traders, using sophisticated technology to generate pricing models. They have more ability to analyze the markets. You could follow them.

'I would say that if you are looking to go into business in this industry, then have a look at what the proprietary trading companies are doing. Most are arbitraging one month against the other. Sometimes it is European stocks against American stocks – they have all kinds of empirical data to measure that.

'It's very difficult for a part-time trader to make money. Studies have indicated that at firms like Lind-Waldock 85–95 per cent of customers lose their money. First, they are starting with limited capital, around $25,000. Secondly, they generally give up the edge getting in and out of the market. They have to pay relatively high commissions. The deck is stacked against them. So if you are someone like that, what you should probably be doing is trading options, buying calls and buying puts.

'If you do want to trade you should be doing it full-time. It's very tempting, because the markets look easy – they are seductive. It's much better to be associated with a successful trading firm in an office where there is lots of information and you can see how people are doing. It's those trading houses that are in Greenwich, Connecticut or New York City where the traders do well.'

TRADING TACTICS

- Formulate a strategy for risk management, that is how can you reduce the impact of a negative move.

- Would you be suited to spreading to reduce risk?

- Your first loss is usually your best loss.

- Progressive trading: one bean at a time.

- You are only a good trader if you can make money out of it.

- It takes discipline not to trade, and not trading is often the most profitable thing to do.

- Exiting – is the pain too great to stay in?

- It is not a question of being smarter than the market, so don't let ego prevent you from taking small losses.

- Find successful traders and copy them.

- Don't be seduced by the market into thinking trading is easy.

4

Jon Najarian

'THE REASON WE ARE
DRAWN HERE IS THAT WE
WANT TO MAKE MONEY.'

TRADING TOPICS

- Joy and tenacity in trading
- Mentors
- Competition and responsibility
- Disciplines
- Insuring against being wrong
- Playing high-percentage plays
- Making luck
- Entry and exit timing

*(Readers unfamiliar with options may wish to read
Trading Appendix 1 on options before reading this chapter.)*

Six feet tall, a statuesque physique and bald save for a pony tail – that is Jon Najarian on the outside. Opinion is divided whether he looks more like Arnold Schwarzenegger or Steven Segal. In the pits he dons a trading jacket with a 'Terminator 2' badge, and 'Arnie' looks worried.

Jon Najarian's office was cluttered, yet spacious. His leather chair, in front of an over-sized computer monitor, had its arm-rests ripped and clawed open, revealing the creamy foam underneath: 'was this due to boredom, or a more interesting emotion?' I wondered. On the walls were numerous awards and photos; a collage celebrating life, family and success.

In 1989, Jon Najarian formed Mercury Trading, a designated primary market-maker responsible for maintaining a market in stocks for which it had been designated. Two years later, it reported a return on capital of 415 per cent. Today it is the second most active market-maker on the Chicago Board Options Exchange (CBOE). Appropriately, the company was named after the Roman god of commerce and protector of traders.

Mercury specializes in bio-tech, hi-tech, healthcare and gaming stocks. It makes markets in 60–80 options on stocks. Income stems not only from market-making, but also from placing directional trades. If it is a busy day, Mercury executes about half a million shares and ten thousand options contracts, about $60 million worth of securities products. Mercury is expanding into other exchanges, such as the Philadelphia Stock Exchange, and other products, such as currency options, real-time data provision, and money management.

A brief history of Dr J

Released by the Chicago Bears as a linebacker in 1981, because a certain Mike Singletary was drafted into the team, Jon Najarian clerked for his agent at the CBOE. The agent knew professional athletes would be aggressive, competitive and quick-thinking, the traits needed to survive on the floor at one of the world's largest and busiest securities exchanges.

Soon thereafter, Jon's agent informed him that he didn't have what it takes to become a trader. Consequently, Jon Najarian decided at that moment that he definitely wanted to become and succeed as a trader. Released by his agent, Jon Najarian worked for free for a position trader named Tom Haugh in exchange for tutoring. Tom Haugh soon became Jon Najarian's mentor. They remain close friends to this day. After four months of running orders and learning spreading from Tom Haugh, Jon Najarian joined LETCO, (the biggest specialist firm at the CBOE) as a partner with Lee Tenzer. Then, in 1983, Jon Najarian went to the floor of the CBOE, for the first time as a floor trader. He went right to the center of all the action: 'Big Blue' – IBM – was the most active equity option in the world. He remained there until 1989 and the birth of Mercury Trading.

Man cannot do but one thing

Jon Najarian qualifies as a Super Trader for more reasons than those described in Chapter 1 of Rubenfield's excellent book, *The Super Traders* (1992). At the same time as Jon Najarian formed Mercury, he also formed the Professional Traders Institute, with Tom Haugh. They act as consultants to foreign banks and large companies as well as providing seminars to individual investors. Jon Najarian is also regularly asked to give speeches on derivatives, trading, the industry and OTC products. He appears frequently on Financial News Network's weekly option report with Bill Griffith, and also appears on CNBC, WCIU, Fox TV's 'Fox Thing in the Morning'.

In 1994 Jon was elected to the CBOE Board of Directors and named co-chairman of the marketing committee. Because he had insufficient demands on his time (!), Jon Najarian also created Options News Exchange (ONE), a real-time audio-based information service.

Finally, 1997 saw the launch of 'Dr J's Planet', an internet site (http://www.drjsplanet.com) designed to provide off-floor traders with on-floor information. The site offers a wealth of quality information and I highly recommend a visit.

Addicted to trading

I have found it to be a common trait among the great traders that they all love doing what they do. They want to be in the game. Their addiction and obsession gives them a vitality, a purpose, in the same way wind gives sails a purpose and vitality.

'I think you have to be comfortable doing it. If you are not comfortable doing it, it is probably not going to be your lifetime career, it may be a short career. There are a lot of traders talking about, "when I make it I am going to live on a beach and run a jet-skiing company or run a tanning company". I could never do that. I am addicted to trading and

> **'The exciting part for the trader is being involved.'**

I need to see the market and trade. I am not addicted like a gambler is addicted, like I have to be at the table. But I have to be in the game. I couldn't just oversee trading, I have to trade myself. That's the exciting part for me.

'I would like to think I am a reasonable manager of people, but if somebody offered me a job as a manager for the same money I make now I wouldn't take it because I want to trade. The exciting part for the trader is being involved.'

Notice that Jon Najarian does not mention money as being the source of his joy. He loves the game for itself. If this is how you feel about trading, then you are in a fortunate minority. If you want to test how you really feel about trading, try to write down ten things you enjoy about it. How quickly these come to mind and what they are will indicate just how much you really enjoy trading.

Tenacity: in pursuit of the dream

We ought not to think that Jon Najarian has had it all plain sailing in trading. There have been times when he has not enjoyed trading. There have been times when he has had to rely on his tenacity to see him through.

'When I first started out it occurred to me that trading may not be for me. I felt it was very confusing, trying to figure out derivatives trading. Derivatives were a problem for me. I had never had any background in it. To figure out how companies were pricing things, how they were responding to requests for bids and offers from the broker was difficult. So the first three months in the business were very frustrating. I did not understand what was going on in derivative pricing.

'But as I picked up on it the light came on. I suppose a little bit of that is the work ethic and problem-solving which I have always been good at. The work ethic came from my family and problem-solving came from working with problems all my life. I like detective work. Ever since then I haven't looked back; it's been great. Of course, you always learn different ways, better ways to do things. It's an exciting job, I love to come to work every day. I am a lucky guy.'

> '**Unless you are willing to bang your head against the door until you break through, you are not going to make it.**'

Jon Najarian is where he is today not only because he naturally enjoys what he does, but because having discovered trading, he had the tenacity to pursue it. It is a lesson for us all, when we are faced with tough trading times.

'The frustration was that I didn't have a teacher when I first came into the business. My sports agent was supposed to be my teacher. He knew almost nothing about real trading. He was only in it for the tax breaks. When those tax benefits went away so did he. So when I was on the floor there was no one to teach me. Listed options were new enough that the people who knew about them did not want to teach anyone because that was such an edge.

'When I finally found someone who knew about options I told him I would work for him for free, just to get my foot in the door, just to learn how to do it. That is when the light came on. But I think you do have to have a determination whether you are a man or a woman. Of course a woman faces greater barriers; on our floor only 2 per cent are women. On most US trading floors there are very few women and so I am sure women have a bigger barrier. Also, no one wants new competition. No one wants to build up their next competitor. Unless you are willing to bang your head against the door until you break through, you are not going to make it.'

Trading like the greats: do you need a mentor?

Many great traders have a mentor on whom they model themselves. But that begs the question, what kind of mentor is best?

'My experience is that the hottest person on the floor is just about the worst teacher. They may be very bright and be able to do it for themselves but they are unable to teach. So I would look for traders that are successful but not for the hottest. Generally, the hottest have such huge demands on their time that you just can't get near them. If I had my choice, I would go to a relatively undercapitalized person who has had to learn all the different ways to trade using little capital. Bank traders have the luxury of having almost unlimited capital.

'It is the same with big firm traders – Morgan Stanley, Goldman Sachs, Paribas, whoever has got unlimited cash. It's easier to do their end of the job because they have never had to have the discipline of a strict limit to how much they can trade with. For that reason I would look for those with limited finance rather than unlimited financing; probably not the hottest trader on the floor but the trader that is just steady.'

Newsletters: substitute mentors

All is not lost if you cannot get a mentor. As Jon Najarian explains, there are substitutes for having a mentor.

'In the United States you see a huge number of people who subscribe to a newsletter. Internet chat rooms seem to be a pretty great way for people to talk with each other to see if they find something they mesh with. Not every great trader is going to have a personality like your personality, your investment goals. So getting into these chat rooms is one way to do it.

'Another way to do it is reading books and reading magazine articles to see which trader seems to have a style that would work for you. I think that an awful lot of us have a difficult time seeing how one guy makes a lot of money and applying it to ourselves. But when you finally find a guy or woman who manages money the way that you manage money and deals with risk the way you feel comfortable with, then you have got a better fit. You can't fit a round block into a square hole. I would tend to trade with someone who had a style I was comfortable with because then I am going to like coming to work every day.'

Before you can determine whether the individual on whom you may want to model your trading-self is a compatible trading personality, you will need to ask yourself several questions:

- Do you like to be as mechanical and mathematical as possible in your trading style, or do you prefer a more intuitive feel for a trade?
- What is your outlook period? Are you considering a short-period trade or longer-period investment?
- What instrument would you prefer to trade? Some traders prefer options to futures, for instance.

Your answers to these questions will determine the suitability of any mentor or guru. For instance, I prefer to trade options to futures, based on a combination of technical analysis and supplemented by short-term fundamentals. I would look to my system to indicate closing a position within ten working days of it having been opened. There is no one mentor on whom I would rely for a trading style, but there is an amalgam of three which, when combined, help reinforce notions I may already have had.

What makes a great trader?

Competitiveness

Jon Najarian highlights several traits which characterize great traders.

'When my agent started us trading he picked several of us at the same time because he felt professional athletes would have discipline, would be competitive and they would be outgoing. If you are talking about floor trading it is difficult to be an introvert and be on the trading floor.

'I think he was right. Those are skills I look for in traders that we bring on. Competitiveness of wanting to be on every trade. The discipline of knowing when to cut your losses. Those are probably two of the most important things for a floor trader. But also upstairs [off-floor] the discipline factor is the number one factor which drives people out of my business.'

Floor traders need to be competitive because they are spending hours daily among a group of mainly men, most of whom smell, elbow each other, stand on each other's feet, swear and intimidate. It is their job to bid or offer for virtually every trade. It would be easy to become dispirited.

Discipline

Discipline to remain in the 'comfort zone'

Throughout the writing of this book, one thing has been very clear. Discipline is stated as the number one, most important trait a trader can possess. This is the discipline to do what is necessary, and in trading what is necessary is usually the toughest thing to do.

'Discipline is the number one thing. Discipline is right there at the top because we'll always cut the trade. We'll cut it no matter how much it costs or what potential there was. We will cut it and take the loss and move on. You just have to put on blinders.

'Traders in our firm are told, "forget where you bought it, forget where you sold it, is it a good trade now?" If it's going against you now and is a bad trade, I do not care what you paid, just cut it. The more you trade outside your risk parameters, your comfort level, when you are not in the comfort zone, the market is putting blinders on you and all you can see is the loss and you cannot see all these other opportunities out there. So you get handcuffed and you just ride losers into the ground. Whereas what you need to do is cut that loss and all of a sudden you're back in your comfort zone and starting over and can move on to the next trade and try to dig yourself out of the hole rather than having to try to hit a home run to get out of the hole.

'I have got a couple of guys upstairs who are great analysts but cannot trade a lick. It is not because they do not make money when they trade, they make money most of the time they trade, but you can't eat like a bird and s*** like an elephant. So you can't make eighths and quarters and dollars when you're trading well and lose $3 or $4 when you're doing poorly. Even if you are right 70 per cent of the time, if I am making a dollar when I am right and losing $3 when I am wrong, I am never going to get anywhere.'

'You can't eat like a bird and s*** like an elephant.'

As Jon Najarian explains, one of the reasons a trader needs discipline is to be able to cut a loss. This is not only because cutting a loss, while it is still in its infancy, is a good way of avoiding a bigger loss, but also because when you are faced with a snow-balling loss you can become mentally fixated to it. Once mentally fixated to the loss, partly because you are not in your comfort zone, it soon affects other areas of your trading. In other words, a loss in one position can lead to losses, reduced profits or missed opportunities in other positions.

Mental benefits of loss cutting

The discipline to cut your losses short also has an emotional benefit.

'If you get overly emotional, this business could eat you up. It could eat your stomach lining raw. Our guys tend to be emotional, but not about the bad things. They are high-fiving each other, but when we are losing money they are very business-like and cutting losses and moving on.

'It is quite the opposite of what I have heard of. I think it was Jesse Livermore who had a big trader and people said you could always tell when his big trader was making money, because when he was making money he was a real prick. He was saying, "God dammit, damn", he was very short with everybody. But when he was losing money he was cracking jokes and everything was funny. He was so relaxed when things were going down because he was taking his losses. He always said that, "when the market's going against me it's easy, because I am disciplined, cutting my losses, I am having a great time. When the market is going up it's tough, because all the old issues arise about patience and timing, when to pull the trigger, and that's pressure." So for him there was a lot more pressure when the trade was going his way which then made him a p****.

'That's the same thing for us, except when the trade is going against us we cut our losses and we move on. We are probably not as happy. But when the trade is going up we're happy because we're trading and it's going our way. So we are a little different to that trader, but the idea behind it is the same. It is easy to cut our loss because we make it so mechanical and there is a methodology to how we do it that we can move on and make the next trade.'

> *'Every once in a while you burn down the sugar cane crop so you get more ash into the ground and make the ground richer.'*

Consequently, having the discipline to cut losses leads to a greater ease, protects the stomach lining and allows you to move on. As Jon Najarian explains, cutting losses is about cutting pain. It then frees you to get on with your trading once again and jump on to opportunities others may not see because they are still nursing their losses.

So that trader who says, "God, I am a damn fool. It's because I didn't go to church this week, it's because I broke my mum's vase when I was three years old", these people look for stupid reasons to blame themselves, whereas we say, "it is part of the game, it is part of life". Every once in a while you burn down the sugar cane crop so you get more ash into the ground and make the ground richer. You learn from your mistakes. It happens all the time. Sometimes I am learning from my mistakes. I try to learn from them, since I paid for them.'

Despite losing 30 per cent of the time, Najarian is still profitable. I am reminded of Jack Nicklaus's explanation of his golfing success: 'I think I fail a bit less than everyone else.' The emotional energy reserves you will have because you cut your losses can then be put to good use, as Jon Najarian goes on to explain.

'Without breaking my arm patting myself on the back, I also think I am very good when the s*** hits the fan. When everybody else is panicking, that is when I think clearest. Quite frankly, then you are taking advantage of the people who are panicking. Many traders can do that because they are trading within their pain threshold. Everybody has a limit, even George Soros, to how much pain he can take. I do not know anybody who just sits there taking all this pain when they are out of their pain threshold. I do that so methodically when I am wrong, that when other people are panicking I am not panicking.'

You now have at least six good reasons to cut a loss short:

- You may end up facing a bigger loss.
- As you get transfixed you will miss trading opportunities.
- As you get transfixed you may get out of profitable positions elsewhere as a sort of 'compensation'.
- As you get transfixed you may be faced with growing losses in other positions.
- You will tie up capital which could be earning a better return elsewhere.
- You should become less stressed and more calm and in control.

Learning discipline

Jon Najarian developed his discipline in the same way we learn many habits – the association of pain and discomfort with certain actions.

'When you are wrong as a floor trader you are wrong in front of 300 people. When you have to admit it at a dinner party, that is bad enough. But it's worse when you do it in front of, not enemies, but people that will gloat about how badly you are doing because you are their competition.

'For every new trader that comes into the pit an established trader is thinking, "I own a McDonald's and now a Burger King has opened up across the street. They may not be my enemies but they are certainly my competition and I resent the fact they are going after my customers." I am standing there with all my competitors in the pit. We're all bidding and offering, and it all comes down to speed and aggressiveness and who sees the best hedge first, wins, and makes the most money on the trade. So the most difficult thing for me was learning how to make a mistake in front of those people and not let it bother me.

'It's like having a nanny or coach slap you when you do something wrong. You start to reach for this and then . . . slap. Eventually you just stop doing that. That's how I learnt the discipline we use upstairs. You have to get comfortable with taking losses no matter how good you are. For instance, we do 20 000 options contracts a day, on average that is 2000 separate trades of ten contracts a day. Even if I am so great that 70 per cent of my trades are winners, then 30 per cent of 2000 means 600 trades are bad. We trade so frequently that we have to have discipline. The readers, the non-professional traders, will trade two or three time a day if they are active. We trade so much each day that we have to be disciplined.'

Given Jon Najarian's experience, it is little wonder he believes trading disciplines can be learnt.

'I believe discipline could be a learned response. You could teach somebody to do it, but you really have to hammer it into them if they have got a problem – you cannot let them ride it at all. You have to be very, very honest with yourself. The single biggest thing is that they need to have a goal for every trade that they make. So if I do a trade and say I am buying a stock at $30 because I think it is going to $35, then I know what my downside limit is – it is $25 – because if I am going to make $5 if I am right, then I do not want to have lose more than $5 if I am wrong. So if I have a goal which I think the stock is going to reach, then, as a minimum, I set my loss at where I think the gain could be if I am right.'

There are several techniques Jon Najarian touches upon to teach trading discipline. Ultimately, a lack of discipline stems from doing what is comfortable. Imagine you have two mental paths which lead to two different actions. Psychologically, you will be more tempted to go down the path of least resistance, most comfort and least pain. For non-professional traders, this same path tends to be the path of least self-discipline. For instance, they find it more comfortable not to cut a loss than to exit the losing trade. Great traders ensure that the path of discipline is also the path of least pain. This is what happened to Jon Najarian on the trading floor. He soon discovered that making losses in front of so many traders was like a painful slap, and he stopped doing it. He became conditioned, rather like a Pavlovian dog.

Other techniques to improve self-discipline include:

- setting a goal for each trade so there is a point of focus; ensure at least a 1:1 risk/reward ratio
- honesty with yourself: Are you avoiding taking a loss? Are you trying to go down the path of least pain?
- using sheer power of will
- having someone monitor you, so they can try to stop you, for example a spouse if you trade from home.

Perceptions of trading risks

Derivatives are about risk. Risk can be bought and sold like any other commodity. Derivatives are one instrument through which risk is transferred. The great traders have a deep understanding of the nature of risk, but perhaps most surprisingly, are risk-averse; they take out insurance against being wrong.

'I am very risk-averse. You have probably seen on people's walls, "risk not thine whole wad". We always try to position ourselves so that we can always trade tomorrow. That is the single most important thing. Not making money today is not more important than being able to come back tomorrow. We always try to control our risk. We try to set a floor. If I want to be short the market, like in the US I am currently short the market [14 April 1997] because I think they are going to raise rates and that will pressure the market. But are we naked short? No, we are long puts and every day that goes by and the market drops, we buy a ton of calls so that if the market turns and goes up we do not lose all the money that we made by being right. You only get so many times a year to be right. When the Fed increased rates that was a clear signal to get short. We will stay short until they raise them again and see what the Fed says at that meeting. But we always want to lock in the profits so we are constantly rolling down our hedge and never just one way long or short.

> '*Making money today is not more important than being able to come back tomorrow.*'

'We are always hedged when we go into a trade. [A hedge is a position where one position profits if the other position loses. So a hedge can be thought of as an insurance against being wrong. For example, to hedge against a long call, one could sell short a different call or go long a put.] We might be very bearish, like going into the Fed announcement, but we are always in some sort of a hedged trade where if we are wrong we are not going to get killed. And each day we look at the trade both during and at the end of the day. Does the market still agree with our hypothesis? If it does then we stay with the trade and we roll the hedge down. If we thought the market had no more downside and was going to just bottom out, would we take off the puts and stay long the calls? No. Unless we like the market to the upside, we are not just going to say let's take the shorts off the table and let the upside run. We do not trade that way.'

Jon Najarian focuses on the fact that trading is not a one-shot game. In order to be profitable, you have to be in the game. In order to be in the game, you cannot lose everything today. As he notes, he could easily increase his potential profit by taking 'naked' unhedged positions. A hedge is an insurance policy which pays out in case of disaster. The temptation with all insurance policies is not to have them, and so save on the premium. However, that would dramatically increase the risk of not being able to play the game tomorrow. Clearly then, risk management requires the discipline to be hedged.

'We sleep like babies.'

'Many days when placing a spread or a hedge, we think "God if someone had tied me up in a closet we would have made a fortune", because as the stock was falling we were taking profits all the way down. Well, that is just the curse of being a hedger. It is also the reason why we sleep the way we sleep every night.'

Because Jon Najarian knows he has disaster protection insurance, he can be more at ease.

'When you come in after a weekend like this, after the market was down 148 points on Friday, it looks ugly; they were having trouble finding buyers all day. Then, if I am stuck in a position, I could be very panicked. But we sleep like babies. I was in New York and had a great time. In fact I wasn't even on the floor on Friday, because we were set up, had our trade on and we knew the plan would be executed.'

Jon goes on to explain the further benefits of the hedge.

'Sure, there are times when we wished that we were not as disciplined. But more times than not we were glad that we were disciplined. We see so many people bet for home runs by putting all their marbles on a big shot. When we bet on a big move we do it with a controlled amount of risk, even though we are betting for a home run. We are buying a lot of out-of-the money puts and we are selling out-of-the money puts as well as a hedge against the puts we are buying. Sure, we are betting to the downside but we are taking a controlled amount of risk. If we say we are buying some puts for $4 and selling other puts for $2, then we only have $2 worth of risk. So I can stay at the table twice as long. The other guy, who is unhedged, is starting to gag when the market is going against him, but we can stay with the trade longer.'

Since the hedge provides Jon Najarian with a comfort zone, he can be free to exercise clearer judgment. Imagine the last time you were panicked by an adverse price move. Did it ruin your day? Did it plague your mind? Did it affect other trading decisions? If so, have you considered hedging your position? You will of course have to examine the cost elements of hedging and the extent you may wish to be hedged. Further factors to consider in relation to hedging include how the hedge will affect your risk/reward ratio, and when you may wish to add to or subtract from the hedge. Risk is a beautiful thing; with ingenuity you can purchase or sell just the precise amount of risk.

Jon Najarian goes on to provide an excellent example of the importance of hedging. Mercury Trading is the designated primary market-maker (DPM) in the SciMed Life Systems, a Minneapolis maker of disposable catheters. The story Jon recounts occurred on 29 and 30 September 1991.

'The stock went from $88 per share down to $56 in one day. We were short going in and had sold short all day. But also we had had a ratio on of short puts, so as the market fell and got past a certain point we got longer and we got longer and longer at an accelerating rate as the market kept going down. As the market fell we got longer, which of course is the opposite to what you would like to happen. We lost over $1m dollars as the move started and a couple of million dollars during that move. We went back to what we do best which is trading and always setting a limit to our losses. We made that money in a little over two months, just by going back to our discipline.

'As I said, I do not care how much you make today, I want you to be able to make money tomorrow. Well, our traders were going for a killing that day because the premiums were so incredibly high before this earnings announcement that they just sold everything. We can never just buy everything. We always need to buy some protection, but we weren't. The traders who were handling that stock saw dollar signs and figured we can make a million dollars tomorrow on the premium as this thing comes in. The risk/reward ratio was not that good either. Our traders thought the market would go down but they had no idea it could go down that much.

> *'We always focus on "what do we look like tomorrow", not how much do we make today.'*

'This is an example of why even though we think there is an 80 per cent chance of something happening, we do not risk everything on the downside. That is why we always focus on "what do we look like tomorrow", not how much do we make today. We have to worry about tomorrow more than today.'

Risk analysis: treating trading like poker

Since Jon Najarian is risk-averse, he is keen to ensure the odds are as much in his favor as possible before he enters a trade.

'I sleep like a baby because by the time we are into big trades and we have made these trades the chances are that we have done our homework and we are very confident. But if we are wrong, then we are just going to cut it and move on to the next trade.

'Some firms hire professional chess players, professional backgammon players. Our guys tend to be card-counters. I wouldn't say we are gamblers though. If we go to the casinos to play, we are going there to work. We are going there knowing what the odds are. Several of our guys can count multiple decks of cards when they go. They just try to play the highest percentage plays when they go. The same is true here. Our guys are planning several moves ahead and when the trades are coming up, we are counting the cards, we are trying to figure out what the odds really are in our favor. There are a lot of face cards in the deck. That's just the same as Morgan, Lehman and Soly all buying aggressively, and there is a big earnings announcement tomorrow. We think they probably have better information than we have and we are going to take a controlled amount of risk, betting on the direction they are betting on.

'I think there is just as good a probability of a stock going in either direction. We tend to be like card counters in Vegas because we can put the odds so much into our favor when we make the bet because we can look at the charts like a long-term trader and see what the pattern looks like – does it look like it has more on the upside than the downside? But that is not enough by itself. Every ship at the bottom of the sea was loaded with charts. So we do not trade strictly off the charts.

'The next thing we look at is the buyers and sellers. Again, on the derivatives side we see Salomon, Morgan Stanley, Lehman, NatWest buying, buying, buying a certain stock and we know they are betting on the upside too. So we are reading all these tea leaves as well. We see that the chart pattern looks good, institutional buyers are coming in – is there anything in the news? Are there earnings coming up? Has anybody commented on it favorably? Is there a new product coming out? Is there a lawsuit pending? We look at all those things so that by the time we actually place the bet we probably have a huge edge because of all those factors we looked at, that our winning percentage is off the charts. Most people do not have the benefit of seeing all that information so what they have to do is give themselves the chance of being as right as possible.'

> **'Every ship at the bottom of the sea was loaded with charts.'**

Few people would associate such a risk-averse, belt and braces approach, with a trader, let alone a great trader. However, risk-aversion and caution are the hallmarks of great traders. It follows from this, that when Jon Najarian does enter a trade he wants the upside to be far greater than the downside, even if the downside move is highly improbable.

'The worst I do is a 1:1 risk/reward ratio. Most of the time I want a 2:1 or 3:1 reward to risk ratio. So if I think it could go to $35, then I sell at a loss, if I am wrong, at $29 or $28 so that I have a multiple risk/reward ratio on the upside. If I am wrong I cut the trade and move on.

'You cannot be willing to say I am going to ride this stock down to $20 if I am wrong, but I am going to make $5 if I am right. If you do that kind of thing, you are just not going to be in business very long.

'I would never put a multiplier on the risk to the downside. I would never say that although there is $5 on the upside, I am so confident that I am willing to take a $10 risk to the downside. It would not be an acceptable risk.'

Exiting a trade: triggers and targets

Many traders focus their energies on trade selection and neglect to consider when to exit. It is as if they expect inspiration from trading heaven to tell them when they should close a position. Knowing when to exit a trade is just as important as knowing when to enter a trade. For Jon Najarian, the reason for entry and the reason for exit are very closely linked.

> *'What is the "trigger" that makes this trade make sense?'*

'Once the event we have been waiting for occurs, we get out. What is the "trigger" that makes this trade make sense? If the trigger is earnings and the trigger occurs then "boom" I am out, if I do not have any other reason to be in. If it is the product announcement or exploration or mutual fund inflow of money that will push the price up, then as soon as I get that information, I am out. Otherwise I have no edge any more.

'I do not buy a stock based on what I read in *Forbes* or what I read in *Business Week*, although they are good publications and they give me information. I put the information together to find the trigger. What is going to drive this stock to move? If it is an analysts' meeting, a conference, whatever, once that news comes out, great, then I am out, unless I have a new reason to be in the stock.'

The concept of the trigger applies even if the stock has not reached its target price. That is when it is most difficult to apply the concept. Disappointed, if a stock falls short of your expected target, there is a temptation to avoid closing the position by judiciously re-interpreting the trigger and convincing yourself that either the trigger has not yet expired, or there is a new trigger. You need to be aware of this likely psychological shortcoming so that you can avoid it. The trigger ought to be part of your trading plan, as Jon Najarian explains:

'Fewer and fewer traders trade by the seat of their pants and the traders that do tend to be futures traders. Traders that trade derivatives tend to set up scenarios in their heads that the stock will appreciate or drop for whatever reason. They then set up a gameplan to deal with the cards that are played – the chart pattern, the firms recommending it, all these different reasons. They then have more and more reasons to bet on one side of the market than the other. Then they decide how to make the most controlled bet they can.'

One problem many traders have is knowing whether they are exiting prematurely, and whether a loss they may have on paper may turn around in due course. Jon Najarian resolves this dilemma.

'It goes back to "target trading". If this trader had a game-plan and a target for the trade, then he is not cutting his loss short, he is cutting the trade. If I think a stock is going to $35 and I cut my loss at $27, I am not just reducing my trade at $27, I am cutting my trade at $27. I am cutting my loss. Now if the situation changes and I had a new impetus that could drive it higher, would I get back in at $28? Sure. But I am not just going to buy it because it is cheaper at $27, or slowly scale out at $27.

'Likewise if I buy an option for $4 and it slips to $3¼ and my target on the upside is $6 and on the downside is $3, then when that option gets to $3 and nothing else has changed in the world to change my mind – I am out. I am not just reducing the number of options I am holding; I am out of those options. I am trying to get out, cut the loss and move on. I would rather

'I would rather deal with one mistake once rather than the same mistake over and over again.'

deal with one mistake once rather than the same mistake over and over again. We try to cut the pain and get out.'

So Jon Najarian cuts his trade if his downside exit target is hit. He won't scale out, because it would not make sense to scale; he has a target, it's hit, he gets out – it's all or nothing.

You make your own luck in this game

A perennial query among traders is the role luck plays in trading. How much of last year's profits were down to good luck? What then if my luck changes this year, am I likely to lose? Jon Najarian is sure luck plays a part in trading. However, for him luck is not controlled by the fickle will of providence, but rather is the product of good planning and forethought.

'Luck plays a big part. Some traders are just unlucky. Part of it is taking responsibility for yourself: "I got hit right at the opening", blaming the alarm clock, blaming the wife, blaming the kids instead of taking responsibility yourself, "of all the days for this to happen, it had to happen IBM earnings day or expiration day". On the one hand that is luck, yes, but it is also not taking responsibility.'

I am reminded of Albert Ellis's famous quote, 'The best years of your life are the ones in which you decide your problems are your own. You don't blame them on your mother, the ecology or the President. You realize that you control your own destiny.'

'There was a man who managed clearing firms down here who told me that he asked every trader that came, "Do you consider yourself a lucky person?" and traders would always say, "What do you mean lucky?" and he would ask, "Do you think you are unlucky? If you are walking down the street does the bird crap on your shoulder rather than hitting the guy next to you? Does your umbrella open and fold and fly out your hands? Does the bus splash you?" If these things happened to you, he wouldn't clear you. He would say you make your own luck

'If you are walking down the street does the bird crap on your shoulder rather than hitting the guy next to you?'

to a certain extent; you don't stand right next to the damn puddle. Granted there is little you can do about the bird flying overhead. But if the bad things are always happening to you, it is probably not luck; it is probably that you put yourself in positions that they can happen to you.

'There are negative things that people do to themselves. Do I think luck is involved – absolutely. The danger of a self-made man is that he worships his maker. I think there is a certain amount of luck in the things we do. Me buying things at just the right time – maybe it was my ego, maybe it was my luck. If I have a big ego, I think it was my skill; if I look at it in hindsight, I think, "gosh I was lucky". We would rather be lucky than good.

'People have to be willing to take responsibility for what they do. It cannot always be, "well this guy came in and screwed me out, then I couldn't get my stock out and that is why I am this long this morning and the stock is opening down $10". That is not an acceptable excuse. You have to be able to say, "I did this because this happened, and then I was wrong and I took my loss". That is what we want to hear when we are backing traders. When we've got traders that are in trouble, they are usually doing the opposite. They are trying to blame everybody but themselves. So the responsibility thing is a big thing. Usually, if in the first few months in a trader's career we are seeing a pattern of him or her blaming somebody else, then the chances are they are not going to make it. We red flag them and watch them very closely.'

Think of the last three times you had a trading loss. What was your reaction? Did you start blaming anything or anyone other than yourself? If you did, then the chances are you have not yet accepted self-responsibility in trading. Without this responsibility you will fail to analyze the causes of your losses, and so, more importantly, fail to remove those causes. Ultimately you will be losing more money than you need to.

Jon Najarian believes that the reason some people are apparently unlucky is because they want to fail. They may have subconscious reasons for wanting to fail and these reasons then manifest themselves through apparent bad luck.

'The reason we are down here is that we want to make money. Some people have guilt about various things in their lives – they don't know if they deserved it, they do not know if they are smart enough to be doing this or whatever.'

To improve your luck, Jon Najarian would advise that you first need to ensure you want to win. Are there any reasons why you may not be comfortable with trading success? Secondly, you need to anticipate things which could go wrong. For instance, have you paid your subscription to your data provider? Have you recently backed up data files?

The patience to wait, the courage to exit, and knowing the difference

In one sense success in trading is only about timing. It is about timing your entries and timing your exits. The problem of timing is one of decision-making and judgment: how do you know when is the right time?

'Timing and patience are very similar, certainly related. Timing: how quickly do I take my profits? It goes back to what is my goal for this trade. In the Gulf War, I was trading IBM. I had thousands of out-of-the-money calls in IBM. They were expensive because there was all this uncertainty ahead of the war and uncertainty brings volatility and option premiums up. But I put myself in a lot of spreads and instead of just making a $\frac{1}{2}$ point all the way up for this $15 run in the stock, IBM opened up $15 and I might have had to sell millions of dollars worth of stock. Instead of making millions of dollars on the trade I probably would have made $50,000 because I would have sold every $\frac{1}{2}$ point all the way up.

> 'The only thing bottom-pickers get is sticky fingers.'

'There are times when the market is creeping up and creeping down and then you do have to be patient and wait. The only thing bottom-pickers get is sticky fingers. My brother Pete is one of our traders and he is very disciplined and his timing is quite good. One of the things he uses is that he reads the other players in the pit and sees where they are in their game-plan. If they are really panicked and they are short, then he will wait a little bit before selling because they are going to push prices up. On the other hand, if he was short too, he is going to be very impatient and pull the trigger right now because he knows the other guys in the pit are short too and he needs to cover. There is a time to be patient and there is a time for impatience, and you just have to know the difference.'

The obvious question to the above response is 'how do you know the difference?' Jon Najarian believes an important part of 'knowing the difference' is keeping to your trading plan.

'Partly it is experience and partly it is sticking with your game-plan. You would be shocked how many professionals take the time to set a game-plan and then do not follow it. Then that is just stupid. We are not brilliant so we are going to stick with our game-plan. We are going to put the odds in our favour as much as we can and then we will stick with the plan that we set. We will make adjustments to the plan sure. If earnings are coming out and I think that is what is going to drive it, and instead a take-over rumor comes out, then that is a whole new set of inputs and basically I strategize and re-price my targets and then stick with that game-plan.'

> '*There is a time to be patient and there is a time for impatience.*'

So, while it is all right to make 'mid-trade' adjustments to a trading plan in response to a new set of inputs, the best way to ensure good entry and exit timing is to have thought about it in advance, incorporate it in your plan and then stick to it.

TRADING TACTICS

- If you are not comfortable trading, then it is unlikely to be a lifetime career.

- Trading will not always be fun. Sometimes you will need tenacity to see yourself through the hard times.

- 'Mentors' should be traders that are not the 'hottest'.

- Find traders in newsletters, magazines, internet chat rooms that manage risk and money like you do.

- You are solely responsible for your positions. Once you appreciate that, you can start to eradicate the causes of your losses.

- You can't eat like a bird and s*** like an elephant.

- Losses: stay in the 'comfort zone'.

- Losses cause more losses in other positions.

- Cutting losses releases emotional energy.

- Discipline: set a goal for each trade.

- What is the trigger that makes the trade make sense.

- Great traders are risk-averse. They protect against being wrong.

- Are you making good or bad luck?

- Are there any reasons why you may not be comfortable with trading success?

- Improve your timing by sticking to your game-plan.

5

David Kyte

'I DON'T COME TO WORK
TO EARN A LIVING, I COME
TO MAKE MONEY.'

TRADING TOPICS

- Enjoyment as a precondition to good trading

- Learning to push your luck

- The qualities of a great trader

- Handling losses

- Handling profits

In researching this book, I asked numerous traders 'whom should I interview, who are the biggest, most successful traders in the City?' One name was repeated far more than any other. That name was Kyte.

When only 24 years old David Kyte formed his own trading company with a mere £25,000. Today, at 36, he is the chairman of the Kyte Group Ltd and Kyte Broking Ltd, supervising gross profits running into millions. None of the boys on a school visit to the London Stock Exchange half a lifetime earlier could have predicted this path for their contemporary.

David Kyte is quietly spoken. This was not what I had expected of a man whose work involved being surrounded by competition. He speaks in restrained public school tones (which may or may not say a lot for grammar school State education) and seems subdued in manner and deliberate in speech. Here is someone who regularly spends hours shouting and who annually risks millions of dollars. Yet, as is often the case with a man at the height of his profession, he exemplifies calm and control. He is moderately above medium build and slightly taller than average height. His hair is short, French Foreign Legionnaire in style. It is a common misconception that young self-made multi-millionaires are readily discernible by their appearance alone. But in fact it is they who are the least readily discernible, for they have nothing to prove.

It is difficult to think of a more central and convenient location for a group of LIFFE traders. The Kyte Group is barely a minute's walk from the LIFFE building. Part of a relatively small pre-1980s office block, the Kyte offices are necessarily unassuming. Upon leaving the elevator on the second floor, a discreet Kyte Group logo points in the direction of the reception area, which is small and functional, almost dental. It has the ubiquitous 'laddish mags' on male grooming, soccer and women and surprisingly little financial material.

David Kyte's office is through just another door in a series of doors along a narrow corridor. It is glass-fronted with venetian blinds affording some privacy. If offices in any way mirror the professional stereotypes of the individuals who use them, then I was receiving conflicting signals. This is not Gordon Gekko. The office is not designed to impress. It is small, sparsely furnished and practical. It is there solely to serve a purpose.

Behind an uncluttered, unmemorable modern desk, on which there are two monitors and two phone handsets, is a shredder resting on a plastic bin. Above this are several photos including one of Kyte meeting the Queen, adjacent to which is a photo of Kyte meeting Bobby Charlton. Although framed, they conveyed an impression to me that they had been tacked to the wall almost as an afterthought, perhaps in an attempt to resolve the conflicting desires of pride and nonchalance. In the minimalist and pragmatic decor, Kyte revealed more of his personality than he intended.

The making of a great trader

'[My interest in the markets] dates back to an economics "A" level school trip in my lower sixth. I was about sixteen years old. We went to visit the London Stock Exchange; at that time there was no futures exchange in London. Just the fact that there were opportunities to create wealth in a seemingly easy manner sparked my interest and everything carried on from there really.

'I did nothing about it initially. That's all there is to it. The visit had created an interest. I went to do accountancy after my "A" levels, but after a year decided it was not for me. I started to look around for opportunities, of which there were far more then than now. Eventually I got a job in a firm of stock jobbers in 1979; I was just a clerk in an office. It was a standard school-leaver type job in a firm called Smith Brothers, which became Smith New Court, now Merrill Lynch. I was a typical pushy young man; "I want to get on to the Stock Exchange floor", "Sorry we're having a rough time at the moment, there are no vacancies at this time", "Well I really want to go, I'm fed up in the office and

'There were opportunities to create wealth in a seemingly easy manner.'

doing clerical work, this really isn't for me". After three months of this I took a job at a firm of stockbrokers, Gilbert Elliot. They gave me the opportunity, in January 1980, to become a "blue-button", which is a dealer's assistant on the Stock Exchange floor. I stayed there until I went from being a blue-button, became a dealer in the Stock Exchange to a trader on the floor.

'Like most people, the drive was to get a greater salary. You hear about all these rises when you're younger, certainly when I was younger, about people earning a fortune. You hear about stock-brokers living in their lovely houses, and they all made their money trading shares, and that was what attracted me in the first place. Then, after becoming a Stock Exchange dealer within the same firm, I was thinking this is great; I'm checking the prices all the time, deal-ing and improving, but I want to get the orders in and create the brokerage (earn commission through buying and selling on behalf of others), which is how your income is derived. I want to be in com-mand of my own destiny. I don't just want to be checking for someone else. So I went to the office, started speaking to the clients, and getting the orders.'

The start of LI(F)FE

'I was there for two and a half years when I heard about this new LIFFE market. I tried to convince the partners of the stockbrokers to buy a seat. Unfortunately, they said "it'll never take off, all these fellas with their colored jackets; it'll never work, not in the City of London". So they obviously ducked the issue. I really wanted to get involved and at this time I saw this advert in the *FT*: "company seeks trading skills, LIFFE". I thought it sounded interesting. I had a couple of interviews. No one had experience in LIFFE – it didn't exist. The people who had the real experience in futures were commodity traders in cocoa, sugar, coffee, oil. These guys were the sharp cookies. Stockbrokers were pedestrian by comparison. I managed to get a job, which was fantastic, getting 50 per cent more than I was earning at the stockbrokers. I thought it was great. I was trading up to go on to the floor when it opened in September 1982. I spent the summer trading on the sugar floor just to get some experience and became a blue-button.

'30 September 1982, we were there, all in one pit, there was only one pit in those days – eurodollars. If you made $200 in a day you were a star, if you lost $100 in a day you were a disaster. That was how LIFFE started – two 'f's for the institution and one 'f' for me. I was trading for clients and trying to get some business. They then introduced the short sterling contract soon after and then the three-month interbank rate. Over that period I developed a reputation and interest in spread-trading, which is basically buying and selling one month against another. I was creating brokerage and, from the execution point of view, clients knew they got a good fill. That caught my interest and attracted other people's interest in me. They saw what I was doing and I started to get lots of brokerage from the big houses. It was nothing major in comparison to today.

'Then after about three months I was head-hunted by one of the other companies on the floor with whom I had been dealing. They asked me to join them, which I did, and they doubled what I was previously being paid. Through that period of time we started making prices as well as trading for our own account and doing deals for the client. This enhanced our reputation because it meant we *were* the market, we made the market and we also got the brokerage. If we were 1 bid at 3 whereas others were 1 bid at 4, we would say "Okay, we will work your 2 offer" and we were then 1 bid at 2 offered, so it worked both ways. That worked well, with the client often getting an improvement. After a couple of years of doing that – making good money for the company not only in brokerage but also in the trading account supported by the bonus I received – I thought if I'm any good at this I'd better do this by myself. That's when, in 1985, I became an own account local trader.

'I couldn't afford to purchase a seat because at that time I only had a small pot of money. Seats were £30,000, I only had £25,000, so I needed that as my equity. However, I had an agreement with the original firm, Sucden, with which I went on to the market that I would do their brokerage at a reduced fee and they would give me a seat for a nominal amount. It worked both ways: they were getting something in execution, enhancing their reputation for low cost and also selling me as a product, and I did their business and carried on doing what I was doing at the same time.

'[The Kyte Group] started as me by myself in 1985, then just developed, not really through any particular great planning or idea as to the future. We are now 100 traders strong. We did reasonably well, brought another trader in and he did reasonably well so we brought another trader in who also did reasonably well and so on.

'Initially I was involved in market-making – buying and selling all the time. When you're spread trading you're buying and selling both months, you're trying to take a point here and a point there. Say the market's 1 to 2, we'll try to work things a little bit better than that, and keep notching up $500, a $1000, keep notching, and by market-making give the client the opportunity to get out and at the same time making money for ourselves. If you do 20 trades like that, $500 becomes $10 000.

'[Today] the bond spread trading comes in one week a quarter, so the rest of the time you have to be on your toes – that's at the longer end. At the shorter end you could do spread trading all day every day. At the moment, when interest rates haven't moved higher for such a long time, the volatility tends to be at the longer end.

'[Other than spreads it's] just positional trades we do. When I was first doing spread trades, interest rates were 14 per cent in the US, so the markets were volatile. Nowadays you just don't see that kind of volatility. For one, I think it will change again and when it does I'll go back into the short end of the market. But for the moment at the longer end we look to make more than we lose.

'[A typical day involves] market-making, that is buying and selling all day and trying to build up a position around the market-making. We are always giving people the opportunity to get in and out, but at the same time we are really trying to create something. By creating a market, in and out, we are creating profitability. My profits, 50–60 per cent come from buying at 6 and selling at 8, buying at 8 and selling at 9, and that gives me the opportunity to build up a position that I can really go for, if it goes right. It also reduces the pain when it goes wrong, because I've built up some profits along the way. So I may well be a seller when I'm long the market, but one's a long-term situation and one's a short-term situation.'

It can be difficult making a market and trying to develop a position. If a market-maker wants to be long bunds because he thinks the price is going to rise and he gets a call asking him the price of bunds, he may end up having bunds taken off him. This is because a market-maker is obliged to quote bid–offer prices without first knowing if the caller is a purchaser or seller. The caller can choose whether or not to deal at the market-maker's prices or go elsewhere, but if the caller does decide to deal, then the market-maker must accept the deal at the price he quoted.

You're good because you enjoy it, you enjoy it because you're good

Kyte exhibits the attributes necessary for success in all endeavors in general and for trading in specific. Commitment, perseverance and discipline are second-nature traits. A prerequisite to these qualities is passion for what one does. Kyte is enthusiastic and energized about what he does. Kyte possesses self-belief in the achievement of his goals. When this happens it is difficult not to be passionate. In fact Kyte does not even consider what he does 'work'.

There are two aspects to his passion: what he does and his form of employment. Many people dislike what they do because they are not self-employed and not direct beneficiaries of their labors, and many people dislike their form of employment but not what they do. For Kyte both aspects are synchronized, not through good fortune but through design. As George Bernard Shaw said, "take care to get what you like or you will be forced to like what you get". (1903) Christopher Morley may have been speaking of the same thing when he said, "there is only one success – to be able to spend your life in your own way".

'[Today I work in] any pit on the Financial Futures Exchange. Currently I am specializing in the longer end, ten-year bonds, gilts, bunds (German government bonds). That's where the fun tends to be. That's where the volatility tends to be. I don't come to work to earn a living, I come to work to make money, and to enjoy myself.

'I like the thrill of going it alone. The fact that you're your own boss, in command of your own destiny. It is down to me. Trading is very simple; either you make money or you don't make money. I wasn't depending on anyone else. When you work for someone else, if you make money somebody gives you a bonus and if you lose money somebody else pays your salary. When I was working for myself, it was the ultimate meritocracy, I was worth exactly what I made, no more, no less.

> **'Trading is very simple; either you make money or you don't make money.'**

'The beauty of trading is that if I want to go and play golf tomorrow, I can. And I don't know what's going to happen tomorrow. Whereas for the average person in this country, whether professional or not, their day is the usual same old routine. I think the day you come in and it's a chore, is the day the enjoyment goes out of the window and that's the day I'll probably pack it in.'

David sees himself, with other traders, as a special breed apart – people who don't want to be working on the fiftieth floor of an office block, almost clone-like, knowing their salary when they are going to retire, etc.

'It's like the elite of any profession, take barristers earning seven figure sums, the top traders can earn a lot. Though I doubt whether barristers have as much fun as traders. And then yes, there is pressure and no there isn't pressure. The pressure is intense when it's there but when it's gone it's gone. You can create your own pressures by having huge positions, then you start worrying about what's going to happen overnight, in Hong Kong or Tokyo. But generally you can have control as long as you're sensible. I've got positions on now which if other traders had, they wouldn't be able to sleep, they'd be uncomfortable, but for me, I'm comfortable with it. If I wasn't comfortable I would think twice about it. If I'm relaxed about it then whatever happens, happens. I know what I'm thinking, whether it will happen I don't know, only time will tell. It's something I can cope with. I'm going out tonight with a guy who imports meat, he doesn't want to know that I'm short Footsie and long gilts, he doesn't care.'

Yet for all his passion, Kyte does 'switch off', considering this an important aspect to his work. It is tempting for those passionate about their work to desire to do it all the time, and eventually to become exhausted. Resting the mind and the body avoids this hazard. But they must be careful they do not in fact dislike their work or their form of employment and so convince themselves that they are switching off when in fact they are avoiding what they dislike.

> *'If I wasn't comfortable I would think twice about it.'*

'It is important on a daily basis, to be a good trader, to be able to switch off. If you're struggling on the floor, the other traders will zero-in. They don't do it intentionally, just subconsciously. You just think they are trading against you because you're going through a bad time. You also need to switch off to give your mind a rest. I think that makes for a better trader. Even the Bothams (Babe Ruth) and Richards (Joe Di Maggio) didn't play or think about cricket (baseball) all the time.'

Pushing your luck to make a killing

The great traders are able to push their luck. *If* they are in a good trade, they will not stand in its way. This may well mean buying on extreme strength. They will push for profits, and apply full throttle with confidence.

'One big day I can remember is the 1987 market crash, "Black Monday". I was having a great, fantastic morning. I was thinking I am going to go home, I didn't want to hang around. Then one of my brokers had an error, well a dispute, with a House that cost $780,000. It was just as well I hung around to see what was going on. Now, what had been my best day by 10am turned out to be my worst day ever because I was responsible for the whole thing. Here was I, "here you go fantastic", but a couple of hours later it's like, "oh no!". We managed to sort it out, and fortunately I am still here to tell the tale. That tainted my view of brokerage as a business. I'm slowly coming round but you can understand why I am not a great fan of the brokerage business.

'Until 10am I just traded the market superbly, everything I did turned out just right. I was one of the people who managed to get in on the Friday despite the bad weather. It was not that I particularly saw what was going to happen, it was just a wild, wild day, and I called it right. Similarly in 1994, when the market was really wanging around, by which time the market was more mature and so I had the opportunity to get in and out in larger size, I had a couple of very good days.

'I think in some respects it's a matter of "make your own luck".'

'Those great days and trades weren't luck. I think in some respects it's a matter of "make your own luck". If you buy near the bottom of the market, it's very easy to get out soon thereafter. If you hear, on the bunds, the market's fallen to 47 with a low and I bought at 50, most people get out at 52, in and out. That's your luck for buying at 50. You make your luck by pushing it, and if it goes from 50 to 60 to 70, then maybe you get out at 80. That's pushing your luck. And that's the difference between a good trader and an average one. Pushing your luck, by, if you're fortunate to get into a good trade, just keeping going and trying to squeeze every last penny out of it. It's not just waiting to see what happens, it's also having a feel for what will happen.'

Traders quote points to each other and not the big figure. For instance, if the $:DM rate is DM 1.7417–1.7420, then the big figure is DM 1.74 and the points are 17–20. DM 1.7405 is '05' (pronounced 'zero-five') and DM 1.7400 is 'figure'.

'You don't stand in the way of a train that's going at full steam.'

'You don't stand in the way of a train that's going at full steam. It's all right to stand in the way of a trade running out of steam, but if it's going at full steam, get on it, have a ride, but the train is not going to go on forever, eventually it's going to start going uphill and slowing down, and you have to say I want to get off here because when it starts rolling back down the hill it's going to be coming back at a similar pace. That's when it's right to be a contrarian (someone who holds a polar view to that of the majority). It's knowing when. I don't really analyze it, but it must be that I get it right more often than I get it wrong. That's why I'm here.

'If you buy at 10 and it gets to 20, should you get out, or should you say, "it's reached this target rather quickly, I'll sell half and push the other half to 30". At times you might say, "I'll get out at 20 and if it goes to 30, well hey". It depends how you feel.

'Scalpers see a small profit and they take it. It's not that they are bad traders, it's how they trade. There is a difference between somebody who goes from one step to the next, from one level to the next. I think you either have it or you don't. You can't teach it. It is either in your system or it isn't.'

When he's in a good trade, (i.e., one which shows a strong profit on a sound advance), Kyte will not get in and out of the trade all at once. He scales the amount of money risked in accordance with his perception of the probability of further profits. This way he is pushing for profits and increasing them proportionately with the advance.

If a trader buys at 15 aiming for 20, and the next day the price jumps to 20, he may well buy more at 20 aiming for a final target of 30. This is where the trader needs speed and flexibility of mind and decisiveness. A trader cannot afford to procrastinate or to be stubborn.

Of course this means Kyte is willing to risk a large proportion of his equity on one trade. Kyte does not follow the conventional rule of diversification and allocating a maximum percentage of his equity to any one trade (usually 5–10 per cent). For Kyte, there are no rules; if the trade is right then it is right, and the great trader will nail it.

The qualities of a great trader

Results

For David Kyte, the prime quality of a great trader can be encapsulated in one word:

'Profit. Greater the profit, greater the trader, it's as simple as that. There are no great traders out there unless they make great profit. Take cricket, the great cricketers are the internationals. Those who play for the counties are good, but they're not great. The great ones are Botham, Richards. They are the ones who have done it at the top level. There's no point defining greatness in the market other than by profits. That's the name of the game.'

> **'Greater the profit, greater the trader, it's as simple as that.'**

Whoever has the most money when they leave is the winner. There are no points for beautiful hand signals or colorful jackets – only money.

'Is Botham a "better" bowler (pitcher), or Richards a "better" batsman (batter)? There are lots of people with good technique, but they just don't fulfil it on the big occasions. The big occasions here are when the markets are wild – that's your big occasion. That's when you have to perform, and performance is seen in terms of the money you make. There are a lot of great technical analysts out there, but they're not good traders though. You say to them here's some money, trade it, and they can't make it. They know where to aim the gun but they can't pull the trigger.'

Kyte defines success and greatness in trading solely in terms of money made. After all, making money is the sole purpose for which the trader trades. The most popular alternative definition of trading success is in terms of the number of correct trades made. However, to me, this is a deficient definition, as it ignores the profit motive. What is the point of being correct 99 times out of 100 if you end up making a loss? What is the point of being technically proficient, if your inability to make money means you have to stop trading?

The quick (minded) and the (brain) dead

'Speed of mind is everything. The ability and flexibility to change from buying to selling. Speed of mind, the ability to change your mind, and having the ability to stick with your decision. Push things when you get it right. The larger traders, if they'd bought the 50s we spoke about, Mr Average would be selling 55s, but the good trader will be buying 60s and 70s, maybe not in the same quantity, but he would be looking to sell them all out perhaps at 90. Pushing things as long as they're going his way.'

Another major characteristic of success exemplified by Kyte is leadership. He emphasizes the importance of decisiveness and speed of mind. The trader has to move fast and decisively, yet he has to be open-minded when the time is right to re-evaluate his position. Just as the leader needs courage, the trader needs the courage to hold large positions.

What the Kyte Group looks for in its traders

David Kyte is clear that discipline and commitment can compensate for talent.

'In the people we hire, I am looking for traders who have discipline and physical fitness. People who are committed usually have a good chance of success. If they don't succeed it's not usually for a lack of trying. We don't want the type of guy who turns up late for the cricket team, doesn't come to nets, doesn't concentrate on his batting, and then can't understand why he doesn't get any runs. Whereas if he's got the ability, it's particularly frustrating. You, however, may be the guy who's not outstandingly talented, but you're always on time, come to nets, you get your eye in, know your game. You always get the 30s and 40s, the uncommitted guy may get the hundreds, but he'll get as many ducks. When you look at the averages at the end of the year it's you who's ahead. We would rather have you who's steady and notches up. You'll sleep better. You might not have as much fun, and as many stories to tell, and you may be viewed as boring, but so what? We're not interested in wild cards. We're not interested in the gung-ho and impulsive. We want the stable and steadfast.'

> '**We're not interested in wild cards. We're not interested in the gung-ho and impulsive.**'

Is greatness born or made?

For Kyte the great traders are born not made, they are innately talented. Nevertheless, there is hope in what Kyte says for the innately inept. He agrees that trading improves with experience and that commitment and passion count for a lot. For the rest, I do not think his message is to pack your bags and go do something else. I believe trading discipline can be conditioned. With discipline and a set of trading rules comes self-belief, confidence and ultimately success.

'I think you either have innate skill or you don't. It's just the way you are. I'll look at certain technical matters, but that won't be all-consuming; I like to know what the other people are looking at, then I'll take it from there. I'll look at them, I won't follow them. If it suits me, then I will; if it doesn't, then I won't. I might have an economic view, but they tend to be wrong nine times out of ten! I think the best traders are those who don't read the newspapers, because the newspapers have yesterday's news. You're there, you're creating tomorrow's news, so why read yesterday's? What will it tell you that everybody does not know? You've got as much chance of getting it right as from reading *The Sun* and seeing what way the page 3 girl's tits are pointing. Somebody used to say Coronation Street [an English TV soap opera] was good last night, that means the market's going up.

'It's also taking a stock of the flows. Some people are Elliot Wave theorists, some are Gann, some are Relative Strength, Market Profiles, depends on the flavor of the month. At the end of the day what you can't take away are highs and lows. You know that the market is as ever approaching a new high or a new low. It's up to you to see if you can push it through, whether it's a good location to go with the market or to go against the market. It's up to you. It's up to me at the time to make the right decision. You get a gut feeling.'

> '*I think the best traders are those who don't read the newspapers.*'

Kyte is telling us that he forms his opinion from pure observation, and thinking for himself, rather than following someone else's interpretation, to determine what will happen next in the market. Is there a buying weakness at this new high? Are the others edgy? Is the price volatile? Have the bulls run out of steam? Do the bears look ready for a counter-offensive? The way the price has moved and reacted to news, the levels it has reached and the length of time it has stayed there all provide useful market information.

But how do you know when to push your profits? How do you know when things are turning bad? How do you know when to get into a trade and when to get out? As with most individuals who are innately talented, Kyte says he gets a 'feel'. He gets this feel for prices through an examination of a multitude of factors. The reasons for him not using one method exclusively over another are several. First, Kyte himself can affect whether the price will break new ground. He himself is therefore a factor which would not be internalized in the indicators. Secondly, Kyte makes numerous daily floor trades; physical impossibility denies him the opportunity to sit down with a PC and analyze the fast-moving markets. Added to this is a further factor: few would deny that prices are affected by the variable influence of numerous factors, fundamental and technical. Consequently, it makes sense that the starting point for attempting to predict future price movement is an examination of the various indicators of these possible factors, and not to focus exclusively on a few.

'There are lots of good traders around, but you are what you are and you can't really change it. I think there is no substitute for experience. And having seen it before gives you the opportunity to take advantage of your experience if it happens again. Sometimes it takes years and years before it happens again. Sometimes you might have forgotten the last time it happened. But, it's something you have within you. Some traders will be highly profitable and make good money, but they will never be great traders because they haven't got it in them.

'There are others as well who put their balls on the line but aren't good traders and they promptly have them taken off them.'

I think everybody reacts. It's how you react that matters. They haven't got the balls to put everything on the line, or a large percentage on the line. They are happy just taking a little bit at a time. And then there are others who push it. There are others as well who put their balls on the line but aren't good traders and they promptly have them taken off them.'

I wanted to know the deep-rooted psychological causes of David Kyte's innate trading ability. Was it childhood experiences, or parental influences or what? I was disappointed not to find out. After several attempts at phrasing the question differently, it became clear my pursuit of this issue would be fruitless. Kyte has a tendency to repeat the same answer to questions phrased too similarly. He will stare at his cross-examiner and leave pregnant pauses which place the burden on the interviewer to move on. It is probably in accordance with his personality that he would not want to postulate romanticized, pseudo-psychological causes of trading ability based upon ill-remembered, idealized childhood experiences. My whole interview experience with David Kyte could be described as a cross between the Sex Pistols and a Nike advert: Never Mind the Bollocks – Just Do It.

If you want to know about losing, ask a winner

It is almost certainly the case that experts in losing are not life's losers, but life's winners. Winners have far more experience of losing, because they get up over and over again. A loser only loses once, that's why he is a loser – he never gets up.

'I'm an expert on losing. I've lost more than most people. I would say I get more disheartened, more pissed off with myself if I lose than I am happy if I make. I believe I should make money, and you get annoyed at yourself if you let your disciplines go.'

As a leader Kyte exhibits confidence in his ability to succeed. As Emerson (1803–82) said, 'self-trust is the first secret of success'. Kyte confesses he gets angry at himself when he fails to make money because he believes he should make money. It is probably the case that his success and his confidence in his ability to succeed feed off each other.

'And yes, you should lose, and I know I can lose and should lose, it's just a question of quantity. If you lose more than you should have done, that's when you get into trouble. It's a lack of discipline in sticking to what you decided you were going to do that causes difficulties. A lot of traders don't focus on their targets and fail to block out emotions like hope, fear and greed.

'You just know how much you were prepared to risk, and it's always annoying when you lose more than you were prepared to risk. Let's say I want to risk £1000 on this trade. If you lose £3000, that was wrong. I only wanted to risk £1000, but I ran it and let emotion get the better of me and knew I was hoping. That's what annoys me, I think "shouldn't have done it, should have stuck to my discipline".'

So, for Kyte, losses are the result of inadequate discipline which leads to inadequate focus on targets and a distraction by emotions. The first step to resolving any problem is recognizing its existence. Many non-professionals deny the existence of a problem. It is a mark of his professionalism that Kyte can speak with ease about the causes of loss, without making excuses. One technique David Kyte uses to correct whatever went wrong is self-analysis and self-talk.

'There are always lapses, it's just a case of correcting them early. We run a school for traders, so they come to us for advice, and we advise them. Who do I go to for advice? I have conversations with myself: "what are you doing? Just get back to basics. Just take it nice and easy." It's a mental battle. You just say bugger it, and walk away for another day. That's the way it goes. It's just something you have to accept. Just make sure you have more good days than bad days. I think it's your losses you have to handle more than your profits. The profits take care of themselves. You can run profits forever. You can't run losses forever. They say the same in every manual you ever read. And it's the people who don't manage their losses that end up going bust. It's just cutting your losses and running your profits. It's a saying that has always been good for me. We try instilling this in our traders.'

> **'You just say bugger it, and walk away for another day.'**

When Kyte does lose money, his positive attitude allows him to walk away. He does not destructively dwell upon his losses, but healthily returns to his trading disciplines. It follows from Kyte's trading method that he doesn't need to be right a majority of times to do well. Since he has the discipline to get out when things are bad and push profits when they are good, he can afford to be right only a minority of times.

Another useful technique in loss prevention involves trade planning and effective risk management. It is when a large part of his equity is involved in one trade that the trader needs courage. If he has made a mistake, he must turn it around quickly. If he has growing profits, then he needs the courage to stand firm. It is far more difficult to stand firm in the face of growing profits than in the face of mounting losses. How often does the failed trader becomes paralyzed in the face of his escalating losses – frozen through fear, greed, hope, pride? And how often, with growing profits, does the trader snatch the silver medal and turn tail? It is discipline in trading strategy, such as pre-defining an acceptable loss, that produces confidence and courage.

'We try and instill in our traders an attitude that is useful. Set yourself a target of how much you are prepared to lose on a daily or monthly basis; when you've lost it, stick to it. Don't hope. There are a lot of people who turn a poor day into a bad day into a terrible day because of lack of discipline. Those are the people who go bust. If it's been a bad day, say it's been a bad day, but I'll be back tomorrow. You can afford to have a lot of bad days if you're disciplined. Don't tell yourself how much you're going to make in a day. If you're making £500, £1000, don't say all right I made £1000 I'm going home now. Go for £2000, or £4000, if it's your day, stay in there. You might make it your best ever day.'

The loser who does a U-turn

Often, if you hold on to a losing position, the volatility often makes it into a profitable one. What should you do?

'It could do, yes. It depends how heavily involved you are. Well, if you buy 50 at 10, are you still happy to be long the next day when they are 5? It depends. Do you average? You may be happier buying 12s and adding to a good position. Everybody differs. The hard and fast rules are that there are no hard and fast rules. It's just quickness of mind and flexibility.'

> *The hard and fast rules are that there are no hard and fast rules. It's just quickness of mind and flexibility.'*

Kyte goes beyond the usual trading rule of cutting losses short because he recognizes that that rule is only a part of the more general rule of getting out of the market if you're wrong. While a paper loss usually indicates one is wrong, it does not necessarily do so. You may be correct about the eventual price movement, but it is taking longer to develop. In that case, if the price moves against you, it may be better to actually buy more at the cheaper price. The trick is to know when the move is temporarily against you and will move back up, and when the move indicates you are wrong. The answer for Kyte comes from his intuitive feel of what is going to happen.

But what Kyte calls a 'feel', is in fact a trading system. His system is more intuitive than mechanical. The important thing is to have a system with which one is comfortable, and to execute it with discipline. There is no one correct system.

Learning to handle profits

It may seem an unusual topic to discuss, after all we all think we can handle winning, but Kyte is quite clear – handling profits is as important as handling losses. Many people, when trading, see a flow of income and treat it as a salary, almost as if they have a right to it.

'Handling profits, setting them aside for when you have losses, it is something I feel very strongly about. A lot of people, they're making money and they go around driving these nice fast cars around the city:

"Look at me I drive a £45k car and live in a £200k house."
"What's the mortgage?"
"£190k."
"Well, what are you trying to say?"
"How well I'm doing."
"And what happens when you lose? The car goes back, the house gets re-possessed."

That's the problem with a lot of people, they're great when they're making money. "Oh, by the way, the tax man needs some money." But they don't think about that. They think they can pay that next year, but next year they don't make any money. The way I've always operated is that the money's there, but until I walk out of here it's not mine, I'm just looking after it for the market.

'Generally, I believe in as high a maintenance of funds as possible. It doesn't have to be in your trading account either as long as it's liquid. It's the people who've spent it all and have the rough ride that have problems.'

On profits, Kyte expands on the usual rule that profits will take care of themselves; profits are not the same as cash. Many seem to confuse the two and overspend, thinking they have a right to a stream of profits. The moral is to spend carefully. The market is a capricious and jealous guardian of her cache – should she grant a loan, she may require full repayment with usurious interest at any moment.

TRADING TACTICS

- Trading should not feel like work. You should be enjoying it. If you don't enjoy it, find out why.

- Remember to 'switch off' and recharge your batteries.

- If you are in a good trade, recognize it and push your luck by staying with it.

- Scaling in and out, depending on the probability of further profits can be a good way to protect profits already made and yet still take advantage of future gains.

- Be flexible enough to change from being a seller to being a buyer.

- Discipline and commitment can make up for a lack of innate talent.

- Observe the market to get a 'feel' of what is likely to happen. Compare it with what does happen and store the experience.

- Trust yourself to succeed.

- Keep a firm discipline when it comes to losing positions.

- Plan a limit to your losses beforehand.

- Losses take more handling than profits.

- If you lose, move on. Focus on the future not the past.

- Be aware of the power of profits to change.

6

Phil Flynn

'I HAVE PROBABLY SEEN
EVERY MISTAKE CUSTOMERS
MAKE; WHAT MAKES THEM
LOSE MONEY AND WHAT
MAKES THEM SUCCESSFUL.'

TRADING TOPICS

- Planning your trades

- Revenge trading

- Keeping a flexible trading mind

- Risk management

Phil Flynn is a Vice-President of Alaron Trading. He 'trades anything that moves'. Having been involved in the trading business since 1979, including a period handling Lind-Waldock's top customers, I felt Phil was an excellent choice to comment on improving trading skills. I was right.

Alaron is a family-owned organization operated by Steven, Michael and Carrie Greenberg. Their father is the legendary Joel Greenberg (who incidentally is interviewed in the sequel to this book). To quote from their brochure, 'the Greenberg goal is to make Alaron Trading the best full-service futures and options firm in the business'.

I met Phil at Alaron's offices. The offices are in a relatively quiet area of town, within walking distance of downtown Chicago and its major exchanges. I was expecting the interior of the offices to be like the locale – subdued, sparsely populated and quiet. In fact, the large interior was buzzing with people and thriving with activity. No sooner would one of them put down the phone and it would ring again. The walls were splattered with graphs, charts and numerical data. In the few hours I was there I sensed this small organization had something many of the large trading and brokerage floors I had visited lacked: there was a rapport among the employees, which filtered into the phone conversations with clients. Work was fun.

Poor planning produces p*** poor, pathetic performance

The simplest and easiest thing you immediately can do to improve your trading and profitability is to plan your trades. Before discussing the contents of a good plan, I am going to persuade you of its benefits. As Phil Flynn explains, not having a plan is a prevalent and basic mistake.

'Most of the new traders read the newspapers. The biggest thing I hear from customers is, "gold can't go any lower, the paper says that it is at a 3 year low". And then they have these perceptions that that trade will be easy money. And now look at gold. [At the time of this conversation gold had broke a three-year low.] So they do not have a plan, they just have a general feeling that due to a situation they read in the paper they want to do this or that. They think, "soybeans look good because of what I read in the *Wall Street Journal*, and so I want to buy soybeans". What I try to do is help them make a plan. "Let's not just buy soybeans. Let's look at this logically".'

Make no mistake, it is not by accident that many individuals do not adequately plan their trades. A lack of planning provides many scapegoats when the inevitable losses occur. If you do not have a plan, you can blame the loss on just about anything. It can even be the dog's fault that you lost money trading – even if you don't have a dog. Without a plan, you do not have to accept responsibility; you don't have to be accountable to yourself. Psychologically that can be satisfying, financially it can be ruinous.

The benefits of planning

Much anxiety in trading, as in life, stems from uncertainty about the future. It is when we do not know what the future holds that we become anxious. Man and woman desire certainty. While a plan cannot predict the future, it can lay down how you will react to the possible outcomes. This is why a plan is so essential. It is a list of strategic responses to events beyond your control. You control the only thing you can control – yourself.

Consequently, a plan removes much uncertainty, which itself is the cause of anxiety, confusion, anger and frustration. A good plan should therefore release psychological energy that is unnecessarily being expended on uncertainties. The flip side is that trading should become effortless, you should be more relaxed and possibly even enjoy your trading more!

Strategically, too, a good plan improves trading. It assists in identifying opportunities and so stops you from chasing the market. It tells you when to exit, so you are not left clinging to the mast of a sinking ship. You gain some control instead of being swept and buffeted around. A plan makes it easier for you to resist the temptation of doing what is comfortable, because in trading doing what is comfortable is often the wrong thing. Think of how many times you have let a loss run or cut a profit short because it was the comfortable thing to do. Eventually, as you get used to following your plan, it will become second nature. So, too, a plan is a means of changing your trading behavior for the better. A kind of trading strait-jacket, protecting you against your wilder emotions.

> *'If you go into a trade with a wishy-washy attitude then you are going to be wishy-washy in execution.'*

Phil Flynn exemplifies the benefits of having a plan. His perspective is quite different from that of the misguided trader. He is in control, anxiety-free and lacks 'negative' emotions such as fear.

'If you go into a trade with a wishy-washy attitude then you are going to be wishy-washy in execution. That is why some plan is better than no plan. You have to look at it like this: win or lose this is a good trade, because if I was stopped out then I was wrong then this is still a good trade. You never make a bad trade. The only bad trade is when you do not follow your rules and you get yourself into trouble.

'I don't care if the market goes up or down. I judge my risk/reward based on where the trendline is, so I know that if I am buying near the trendline and I get reversed, and later all of a sudden it goes back up, I have no problem going back up again. I try to think on a longer-term basis. The reward is not going to be in one or two days. Do not be afraid if you get stopped out at the low. If that is the low you have got plenty of time to get back in. If you look at it from a longer-term viewpoint it makes it a lot easier.'

Elements of a good plan

A good plan should have at least two basic qualities. It should tell you as clearly as possible when to enter the market and when to exit the market. It is a matter of personal choice whether entry and exit signals are based on fundamental, technical or other indicators. Clarity is the key. If your signals fail to provide clarity, you will seize on the ambiguity and fail to do what is required.

Next, you will need to test the plan to ensure that it is consistently profitable. In other parts of the book we will discuss incorporating risk and money management into your plan. As Phil Flynn explains, the plan need not be esoteric and complex.

'What I like to do is to be a trend-follower. That means the ability to determine what the trend is. The easiest thing to try to do is find a long-term trend and buy off the trendline. But the thing is, if the price violates the trendline, you must have the ability to switch to the opposite side. So if I am looking at a trading plan in terms of the entry point, I am looking at the trendline and looking to buy off that. If the price violates that trendline, then I either exit or switch.

'As far as projections go, what I try to do is very simple measurements of past market performance. If we hit one of these points and I have multiple positions, then I take off one contract and tighten up the stop on the other one. A perfect example has been the soybean market. It has been very bullish, but the ability now, even with all the bullishness of the market, to go higher is limited.

> **'The easiest thing to try to do is find a long-term trend and buy off the trendline.'**

'There are, of course, times when the market is volatile and you are going to get whipsawed. That is when you look at the broad fundamentals. Try to look at the market and ask what the market will do next. It is simple and basic, but it is what the average trader can learn from and it gives you a basis to set up your technical strategy.'

Stick to the plan

You will have heard the cliché that to be a great trader you must be self-disciplined. Part of that self-discipline means following your plan once you have formulated it. In other words, enter when your plan signals an entry and exit when it signals an exit. In between, do nothing but observe.

'The other thing about great traders is their discipline, sticking to their plan. What I have done to be more disciplined is to become more mechanical. I take the pressure off myself. I let the markets tell me when I am right or wrong. It becomes a lot more easier if you can make it non-personal. "This is the position, this is the price, this is the target, this is the stop".'

As Flynn demonstrates, one way to achieve the self-discipline needed in trading is to remove the emotions. Write down your plan, do not just keep it loosely in your head. Write down when you should enter and exit a trade. This provides a point of focus and makes it easier to do what needs to be done. Self-discipline is, after all, only doing what needs to be done, when we don't want to do it.

The major pitfall of success: fiddling with it!

Once you have found a plan that works, leave it well alone. Success in trading too readily leads to greed and arrogance – the twin emotions which always surface before a fall. For some traders the reason they fiddle with their plan is more deep-rooted. Subconsciously, traders may feel guilty with their success. 'So much money and so little effort.' The traders and the market often find circuitous routes (for example, by changing a winning plan) to returning the bounty from whence it came. Try to be aware of subconscious conflicts you may have with earning 'easy' money.

For other traders, as Flynn explains, it is the acquisition of an ego that leads them to change a successful plan.

'Probably the biggest downfall traders have is that once they have found success they change their trading rules from what gave them success in the first place. A perfect example is a trader who was a day trader. He started with 50 point stops. These turned to 100 point stops. These then became 200 point stops. I have said to him many times, "I can take any five days of your trading and if you had put on a stop you could have made tremendous money". He had no control over his risk. All he could think was, "I have to be right, I have to be right".

'Probably the worst thing for traders is to have some success in the beginning. It can be their downfall.'

'Probably the worst thing for traders is to have some success in the beginning. It can be their downfall. They get away from what made them successful. They get too big for their breeches. I like to say he was playing the market like a fiddle until he got hit over the head with it.

'I think it is ego-driven more than anything else. I think the hardest thing to overcome in this business is your ego. You have success and you think, "I have got this thing figured out". You start to think, "I got stopped out three times with my tight stop, so I am going to go with my big stop or no stop at all". They go from trading as they did in the beginning, when they traded like scared little rabbits and where they were successful to where they now have no fear whatsoever.

'It is one of the most difficult things – trying to control success. We see it all the time in the sports world. People change their personality.'

Flynn gives us an important warning. As a trader you must be aware of the power of success to change you for the worse and turn you into a loser. For those who have stolen success from the markets, the 'mother of all losses' will chase them relentlessly. The price of success is eternal vigilance!

As Phil Flynn explains, you have to be cautious if you are making money and experience the urge to change your plan.

'The best thing to do when you have a trading plan that is working is to think very, very carefully before you make a single variation. I guess being somewhat mechanical is the best way to avoid that situation. If you change anything that is working, you have to make sure it is not your ego doing it. You have to make a very solid decision that this is to improve the system as opposed to taking bigger risks for the sake of it. Have it written down before you change it so you can always return to the original plan. Test it before you change it. If you think, "hey, I am going to change my system", stop trading completely and paper trade it before you trade it for real.'

> *'It is one of the most difficult things – trying to control success.'*

If you have identified a genuine problem with your trading system, only then is it time to examine ways to resolve the problem.

Finding solutions

'If you recognize a consistent problem with your trading, that is one of the best things that can happen to you. It can then be fixed with flexibility and adaptability. I had a customer who said, "I do not want to use my stops any more because every time I buy I get stopped out". "If that is true," I said, "let us put your buy order where your sell stop is." Something as little as that can change your psychology and give you that little bit extra. So, instead of chasing the market, why not look at things just a bit differently.'

Finding solutions to your trading problems is a lot like finding solutions to any problems you may have. Step away and view things from a different perspective:

● Specify the problem in detail.
● Specify the problem in as many different ways as you can.
● Think of what a solution would look like.
● Think about how you may get from the problem to the solution.

'The best thing to do is to get your mind off it and come back to it fresh. What I try to do is look at every day fresh. Try not to get too high and too low, keep it on an even keel. There are a lot of sports analogies: "take it one day at a time" – but seriously, that is an important key to success. It is very difficult to do. Analyze your mistakes: "this is what I have done, this is what I need to do". Even if you were a zero yesterday, you can be a hero tomorrow. Try to keep an even keel.'

Utilize the power of the mind

The solution to any trading problem lies within you; it is in your mind. To prise the answer from the dungeons of your mind you must be resolved to find a solution. You must also believe you can find the solution. Self-belief in your own abilities together with confidence are the keys to unlocking the solution. Before you even embark upon sitting down to find the answer, remind yourself of successes you have achieved with determination. Know that in the next few hours or days you will solve this problem. Then relax in the knowledge that the task is nearly complete.

As Flynn notes, the mind is a powerful tool at the trader's disposal.

'Look at golf players, one day you shoot an 80, the next you shoot a 120. What is it about the mind? You take one day at a time, so you stay within yourself and do not get too over-confident. At the start of the day I tell myself, "today is going to be a good day". You get yourself mentally pumped up. It is the old PMA: positive mental attitude. You have got to have that attitude, but you have to be cautious, have a plan, and it's when things go bad that you have to keep that attitude.'

Revenge of the trader

One of the most common trading mistakes Flynn has encountered is the desire to wreak revenge upon the market.

'The other most common mistake is "revenge trading". They will get mad and double up. That is one of the hardest things for customers to overcome. When they have had a bad trade they will try to get even with the market.

'You get into a trade, and then you get stopped out at the high of the day. You were right about the trade, and the high was a spike. The market now comes down 200 points, and so now you are mad. You think, "if only the stop were one tick higher or if I had had no stop". Then you think, "I am going to sell this market the next bounce

'Place the trade and walk away.'

it has. I am going to sell it and get my money back." So you sell and double up. And sure enough it goes back up to your original stop and stops you out again. It is human nature, no one likes to lose.

'One way to avoid that is to convince yourself you will only make one trade in the day in that market. That is just another discipline to get away from revenge trading. Place the trade and walk away. I knew a trader that did this. He would do his charts, his analysis, place his order and then the next day look at the paper. He did not know whether he was winning or losing until the end of the day. But that was his way to solve his problem. So you can become a successful trader by taking a step away from the markets.'

Hence, if you find you get itchy fingers sitting in front of a price-screen all day, then don't. The technique Phil Flynn mentions of 'switching off' can be very effective. Most traders feel they have to be in front of the screen, otherwise they are not real traders. That may be so for the professional currency trader, but for the rest of us it is not so. If you have identified a trading problem and the solution is to walk away from the screen, then do it. You are no less a trader for it. In any event, would you rather be a poor trader or a rich Joe.

The flexible mind is the profitable mind

When traders are faced with a loss, they often freeze, hoping things will change, stubbornly ignoring signals which are telling them to exit. As a trader, if you ignore information, your world is black and your finances will be red. Stubbornness, born of hope or fear, will lead to losses. To do nothing despite the information you are receiving can be comforting when faced with a loss. In psychology that is called denial. In the markets it is called suicide. You can hope all you like that a losing position will turn around, but hope alone has yet to cause the markets to move. Faith can move mountains but hope cannot move markets. Your mind controls you, not the markets.

'Because when you get into a position, for instance when you are long gold and gold starts coming down, you have a particular mindset, "I do not think gold is too low". This is the fallacy of "fair price". And I guess it is ego more than anything. Probably the hardest thing to do is stop, change and go in the other direction.

'You say, "hey, gold is at a low price, I have got this trendline, I look at the fundamentals, they are closing a mine in Africa, they are having a war over here, I have to be long gold". And when the market action does not justify what you think the fundamentals are telling you, you say, "even though the price broke this trendline I still think it is going to come back up. I am not going to change direction, I am just going to forget about the trendline." Then what tends to happen is that you end up taking a big, big loss.

'It is getting into a position where you think something has to happen that you become blind-sided and no matter what you are being told by the market, you stay long. Probably the worst thing that can happen to a trader like that is being rewarded. Because somewhere down the road he is going to be slammed.'

You have to be aware of this pitfall. Do not become attached to a view. Remain open to the possibility you are wrong. If you find you are consistently having problems taking losses, then as soon as you open a position, continue on the basis that it is probably wrong unless proven right, and not that it is probably right unless proven wrong. Guilty until proven innocent. You are a soldier of fortune. You owe no loyalty to any position.

Risk Management

Define the downside

Although it is a basic element of any trading plan, few people define their downside. Instead, they focus on how magnificent the upside will be. As a famous New Yorker once said, 'look after the downside and the upside will take care of itself'. After his bankruptcy he truly knew what that meant. Phil Flynn is all too familiar with this attitude.

'The major problem with new traders is their failure to pre-define their risk. They do not know how to admit when they are wrong and they end up staying with the position much longer than they want. When they get into the trade they have an idea of where they think the market is going to go, but they have no idea of how to protect themselves on the downside. Define upfront your entry, your loss order and your profit order.'

Smart risk management means avoiding overtrading

'The other thing they run into quite a bit is trying to overtrade their equity. Like in a $5000 account they will buy 5 pork bellies futures. Just because they have enough margin for the position, they also think it is a smart thing to do the trade.

'You have to ask, "do I want to build this position up slowly, or do I want to be more aggressive and go for it". What I have found is that you can be successful both ways. Some of the traders I have seen, will scale right down, and that can be extremely successful in terms of risk. I think there is not a simple formula. It really comes down to you. If you are looking to make a quick killing, then you want to concentrate your funds and pyramid. But the problem with that is that you could lose a lot more and be out of the game very soon. As far as the risk versus profit potential for the amount of dollar, you can always put a percentage limit on that. You can say, "I will only margin 10 per cent of my equity base".

'The general rule of thumb if you are going to be conservative is that for the amount in the account to the amount of margin, you want to be under 20 per cent or as low as 10 per cent. That will give you the ability to withstand a lot of bad times.'

Flynn is saying that just because you have enough money in your account, that does not mean you should use it all. Keep some of it as a buffer in case things go wrong and you have a string of losses. The key is to stay in the game.

A winning attitude to losses

Phil Flynn, like many of the traders in this book, exhibits an attitude to losses that is rarely found in the non-professional trader. Because his whole perspective is so different he never encounters the difficulties of loss-taking which have to be overcome to become successful.

'It is part of the game-plan. If I am going to be successful, I am going to have to learn to get out of the market with small losses because if I continually end up taking big losses, then I am not going to be around in

> *'Learn to love your small losses.'*

the game. Say to yourself, "that is a good trade because I only lost $2500". That way, you are in control.

'As one trader said, "learn to love your small losses". If you can learn to love your small losses, you are that much closer to a big winning trade. Keep your losses small, but if you learn to love your small losses you can say, "even though I had a loss it was a good trade, because it was a small loss and a well-planned and executed trade". Sometimes, the best trades are not the winning ones that put money in your pocket; sometimes they are the ones that get you out of the market at the right time.'

When faced with a loss, remind yourself of several things:

- Losses are natural – they will and must occur to be successful. Perfection is not an option.
- It is good to take the loss now and have avoided a bigger loss. Profits result from not only how much you make, but also from how much you do not lose. This is rarely realized and often forgotten.
- If you obey your system, you are closer to being a self-disciplined trader, and that will pay off a thousand-fold in the future.
- Ironically, it is focus on your method not on your winnings or losses that will result in profits. By taking this loss you proved your focus was correct.

I am telling you the truth: taking an early loss in accordance with your system is a sign of success.

The missed opportunity that never was

In writing this book three interrelated things became very clear from all my conversations:

1. Contrary to the popular belief among 'lay' people, you do not need to risk a lot of money to make a lot of money.
2. There are low-risk trading opportunities out there, but you need to be patient for them to arrive. Catching the wrong bus, just because it came first, will not get you to your destination any quicker. On the contrary, it will delay your arrival.
3. There are no missed opportunities, because there are ample opportunities all the time.

'Some of the best trades that I have ever made have been the lower-risk trades that have done very well. It is hard to be patient if you have had a losing week or day. I mean being patient for just the right entry point. There are some extremely low-risk movements in the markets, if you have the patience to wait for them to come along.

'Patience is one of the hardest things because you want to make money every day, you want to be in the markets every day. You are afraid to miss the bus. One of the things I always have to remind myself as a trader is that there is always another bus coming down the street. If you miss this one, just be patient because it is coming. If you do not think it is coming you are missing the point.'

> 'Some of the best trades that I have ever made have been the lower-risk trades that have done very well.'

Phil Flynn is saying that patience is an essential element to risk management. Without patience you are likely to take ill-conceived chances and raise your risks. Impatience stems from fear and possibly greed. If you are looking to enter a position, then the fear is of missing an opportunity. If you focus on your system and wait until it gives you the go-ahead, patience will come easier. If you believe in your system and remember only to trade as it tells you to, then you need not fear any missed opportunities.

'There is a fear of missing the trade. You think, "this soybean is coming to the high, but I have to buy it because it is coming to the weekend and it might not rain, and then I will miss it again". You are so afraid of missing the move that you will pay a higher price. It goes up and you keep saying, "I should have bought it". Then you see it going up and you start getting mad at yourself. Then you end up chasing the market. It is fear and anger.'

The fear of missing an opportunity occurs not only when you are looking to enter a trade, but also when you are looking to exit one. When you are in a trade and thinking about exiting you are afraid that you may be selling too early. This is the 'looking back, I could have made more' syndrome. You are so busy looking over your shoulder that you fail to see the gaping hole in front of you.

'As well as learning to love your small losses you have to learn to love your profits, even if they could have been bigger. I think the easiest way to do that is to have multiple positions and ease yourself out, to avoid gut-wrenching decisions. If you have ten positions and you reach your objective, then you could take off half and raise the stop on the other half to protect its profits. So let the other half ride. Always have some sort of objective in mind though.'

Flynn's advice to those who can't help thinking they could have made more each time they exit a position is to scale out of it.

Alaron's web address is http://www.alaron.com

TRADING TACTICS

- Plan your trades, so that you can remain in control, confident and calm.

- Your plan has to clearly tell you when to enter and exit and when not to.

- If the plan works, stick to it and do not change it.

- If the plan does not work, identify the problem and use the techniques outlined to resolve it.

- Be aware of revenge trading.

- Avoid attachment to a position and stubbornness about a viewpoint.

- Risk management: define the downside.

- Risk management: keep spare money in your account in case of a series of bad trades.

- The only missed opportunity is when you do not follow your system.

- Patiently wait for low-risk, high-reward trades.

- The only missed opportunity is when you run out of equity to trade the market tomorrow because you chased the market today.

7

Martin Burton

'IN EVERYTHING YOU DO IN TRADING, YOU ARE BEING TESTED.'

TRADING TOPICS

- Personal trading harmony
- Personality-suited trading
- Stages of planning a trade
- Avoiding 'market chasing'
- Viewing losses properly
- Self-belief and trading courage

A driver pulls into a petrol station. He asks the young, long haired, probably slightly shabby, petrol pump attendant for a full tank. The attendant immediately replies with the total amount payable in shillings and pence. The driver perceives the attendant is quick at arithmetic and offers him a job. That was 26 years ago. The driver was the senior partner of a leading London stock-jobbing firm and the petrol pump attendant was Martin Burton.

Today, Martin Burton is the Managing Director of Monument Derivatives – the firm he formed in 1991. He became a member of the London Stock Exchange at 21 and a partner of Bisgood Bishop at 22. He established Monument after four years as Managing Director of trading at Citicorp Scrimgeour Vickers, where he was responsible for all trading in UK and European equities and derivatives, prior to which he was at County NatWest where he established the derivatives operation.

Monument's personnel are involved in market-making, proprietary trading, derivatives broking, fund management, technical analysis and quantitative research. Martin Burton himself trades futures, options and cash markets. While their trading floor is not as large as that of the big banks, it appears to generate as much noise.

'I have never had a year where I have lost money'.

As he left the trading room to meet me, the first thing I noticed about Martin Burton was his plump cigar. The next thing was the hand-embroidered initials on his made-to-measure shirt.

'I have never, in 26 years, believed we are playing a soccer game that is 90 minutes long. My performance over the long period has been successful. I happen to have been involved in the last couple of years with a small trading fund that is in excess of 50 per cent up. To me there is nothing wrong with making no money in a year, but do I lose lots? I have never lost lots. I have never had a year where I have lost money. That is really a controlling instinct. It does sometimes limit your upside. But that is how good my belief is. I trade within my personality.'

Personal harmony produces better traders

Perceptive traders know that in order to make money it is not only the markets they must handle correctly, but also themselves. How they feel about themselves and the markets will affect two very important things: how they view information they receive and how they react to that information. One thing is for certain, feeling anxious, distracted and annoyed will not help them trade well. The path to successful trading starts well before understanding technical indicators or the meaning of the latest GDP report. The path starts with self-analysis.

'I look at the markets from the macro position down. I also look at myself from a macro position down. It starts at the beginning of the day when I awaken. I immediately have a feeling. I have to feel good about myself. I have to have the right bio-rhythms about myself. How I am in the morning will affect how I dress, how I will be thinking about my processes of the day as I prepare to leave for work. That sets the mental state for how I will be on the day.

'I know that if you are at your best, you will perform. You have to make sure you are at your best because there is a fair chance you will then be at an advantage. But that is why you can't lie to yourself. There is no question of trying to feel good just because you want to trade.'

Martin Burton ensures his mental processes are harmonious, as a pre-condition to market entry. Thus he employs both a personal, as well as market, strategy. This technique ensures focus and therefore better market judgment. Being at harmony with yourself helps ensure you are not distracted or making decisions for the wrong reasons.

'I am not keeping anything to myself. Relationships are good. There must not be anything outstanding in other parts of your life if you are going to trade well. If you are not at ease, if you feel there are other issues outstanding in your life, then you are not in the best position to trade. You cannot have anything that is going to interfere because if it is going to interfere, I bet you it will interfere at precisely the time you don't want it to. It is the way you conduct your life which is the way you trade.'

> *'It is the way you conduct your life which is the way you trade.'*

If traders know themselves, they will be better placed to recognize why they are acting in a particular way, for instance, why they are placing an order despite having doubts. A common occurrence among traders is an urge to close a profitable position when they are feeling miserable or unhappy. They want some gratification from the markets to counter the displeasure in their personal lives, so they take a paper profit they are sitting on. Self-analysis may alert such traders that they are taking a premature profit to make themselves feel better. Honest self-knowledge, through honest self-analysis, may awaken them to their true and subconscious motives for their potentially costly non-trading related actions.

On the same point, there is no value in having a trading plan and not sticking to it. Being aware of your feelings will dictate whether the trading decisions you make are based on your plan and an objective assessment of the information you have, or are based on emotional baggage you have dragged into your trading life from your personal life.

'So, when you are going into battle with the markets, you should not have any weaknesses within your own personality. You even ask yourself, "why do I feel like this, why do I feel so good?" I question myself whether I really feel like I do or if I am kidding myself. Am I on track? But what all that only means is that I am prepared to bet, not that I will bet.

'You move on and look at the markets in the big picture. All of this is background information on whether you make a bet or not. You go down to make a micro bet on an individual stock, but only if you are totally at ease with all the work that has been done before.'

Consequently, it is only after all his self-analysis that Martin Burton decides whether to trade or not.

Not trading can be the most successful strategy

'If I know there is something else that is troubling me more than trading, it is very likely I will not place a bet at all. I will continue to do more work during the day but not place a bet. If you are in control of your emotions, you have an advantage. So, too, you have to be in control of your patience. I can very much identify with the patience of not trading. I do not think there is anything wrong with trading in a very small way just to keep one's hand in. I do not consider that trading. That is just a way of keeping in touch with the market. But if we are talking about trading to make real money, then you have to make sure all the pieces are in place before you do it.

'You do not have to trade every day or even every week. If a reader considers himself a trader and is at ease with himself, then he does not need to trade every day. You are what you believe you are, but obviously you have to have a sound basis on which that is true. I do not believe it is true that you have to trade every day to be a trader. You cannot lie to yourself. If the bets were placed they would be very small. You are constantly building up to make sure that when you do place bets then they are placed when all the other things are in place.'

At first I was surprised that such a successful trader as Martin Burton would advise not trading for relatively long periods of time. But then I realized why that made perfect sense and also why he was the interviewee and I was the interviewer.

> **'You do not have to trade every day or even every week.'**

Since you ought not to trade if you are not feeling 'right', you have to consider methods to control your feelings. Feelings which are most likely to adversely affect your trading stem from unresolved personal conflicts. Conflicts can arise from things such as rows with your partner or work pressure, which distract you when you should be concentrating on trading. It is only you who can identify what these conflicts are and then set about resolving them so that your trading can proceed. You have a strong motive to isolate and resolve these conflicts because your trading edge may depend on it. In the meantime, as Martin Burton says, you do not have to trade; wait until the conflict is resolved and you feel more positive.

But remember, 'you have got to be very positive in your thought process and yet also be humble. You also have to be accountable for your losses and profits. If you try to create positiveness, having been taught positiveness (and I have seen management consultants try to teach it many times), it will not work. They may create positiveness but they have not taught anyone how to take losses, because it does not actually work deep down. I know a person who is totally trained as a top manager, but he is a "created" individual. The trading environment would find him out, whereas business management doesn't.

'There is no hiding place in trading. You have to live with yourself. It is not a question of show, you have to come to terms with yourself. You can't lie to yourself. If you believed you were taught it then you start doubting what you had been taught, whereas if you inherently believe it anyway there is no question of doubting it because it is what you believe anyway.'

Trade within your personality

Trading with a system that does not suit your personality inevitably results in fighting both the system and yourself. Without an appropriate system you will wear yourself and your finances down. It is a little like playing football with someone else's gear on, or going into battle wearing someone else's armor. It is self-evident that even if the football gear belongs to Joe Montana and the armor to Julius Caesar, you will not perform as they did.

'The key thing is that you have to trade within your personality. It may be that your personality is flawed, as indeed I am sure mine is. The flaw in my personality is that there will be times where I may be too aggressive or too quick to react. There is no point in me

> *'There is no point in me trying to play tennis like Bjorn Borg if I am John McEnroe.'*

trying to play tennis like Bjorn Borg if I am John McEnroe. Therefore I try to trade according to my personality, a personality that is capable of being aggressive on occasions or quick to react. To me if I occasionally release anger I am doing myself a favor, even if I am not doing anyone around me a favor, because I am releasing all the poisons I have. Then, as soon as I have released them, I am totally free.

'If you are a certain type of a person, you have to identify what you are. Come to terms with yourself as a personality, genuinely and without lying, and not something you would like to be. Trade with what you are. That to me is a really big key issue with traders. I am what I am and I have no pretensions as to what I am, and I am happy to trade within my own personality. That is a very important point for me.'

'Trade with what you are.'

Your system must play to your personality strengths and mitigate the influences of your personality weaknesses. You first need to ask yourself what are your personality strengths and weaknesses, and what do you like and dislike about trading. For instance, are you patient or impatient? Do you believe in technical analysis? Do you enjoy plotting charts? Do you prefer a diverse or concentrated portfolio?

Next, decide if your system plays to your attributes. For instance, if you are impatient, then when devising your system, you would obviously not be looking at long-term investments. You would want a system, probably based upon technical analysis, that indicates imminent price movements. A system based on projections of likely long-term demand for a company's products is hardly likely to suit your personality and would probably lead to frustration.

A further example of harmonizing your personality to your trading system is, if you dislike examining graphs and do not believe in technical analysis, you should not be spending much time on the ROC indicator as a predictor of price. Or, take another example, if your personality is very risk-averse, you may consider options a better instrument than futures. If you are indecisive, you may want a system which spells out in detail when exactly you ought to enter and exit. If you are not a very quick thinker, you should probably not be an intra-day trader. Finally, if you find you are over-stressed when managing more than, say, three open positions at a time, you would want a system whereby each week you select only the very best trade that is available to you and open no new positions once you reach your limit of three open positions.

Success is in the decision-making

The stages of placing a trade

After self-analysis, identify the opportunity: profit, loss and time expectations

Martin Burton has several layers of thought processes before entering a trade. The first level begins at the start of the day. As was mentioned above, he conducts a self-analysis of how he feels. The next level involves identifying the opportunity and placing the trade.

'You have then identified the opportunity that you believe should be exploited. You then know automatically how much of the ranch you are prepared to bet. When you do that you have an expectation of your profit, you also have an idea of the approximate loss involved when you put the bet on and you go ahead and bet.'

Re-analysis once the trade is opened: profit, loss and time expectations

Once the position is opened, Burton's analysis does not stop there. He then asks again how he feels about the position and his profit expectations.

'There is another layer of mental process. Then I really analyze how I feel about my position. I am not able to analyze my position truly until I have the position. There is then something I can relate to. It is then alive. Once it becomes live I then override that position with another layer of instinct. Then I bring back my expectation of profit and the time that expectation is going to take. I then realize the time that it is going to take to get there is beyond my personality. Therefore although the price is going to satisfy my expectations, it is unlikely that as a personality I am going to be able to absorb that.'

It is significant that Martin Burton concedes to his personality. If a price target is going to take one month to achieve, he may not make the trade because, with his personality, he knows he will have trouble waiting that long. It is being at ease with yourself that produces the best trading results and best judgment. If you are unhappy with a situation, the mind has a funny way of letting you know by curious control of your actions. Traders who are happy keeping open positions for only one week, will soon find excuses to prematurely exit a position which would require three weeks before it would hit their expected target.

Continual re-analysis

If Martin Burton starts feeling uneasy about a position, he knows it is time to re-evaluate. This too is about having a trade with which your personality is comfortable. If the trade is not in harmony with your personality, you will suffer errors of judgment.

'I know that if I am thinking too much about a position, then it is time to get out. I am obviously thinking about it for some reason. Once I am thinking about a position I have to accept I am not going to be too good if it starts to go against me. Unless I can convince myself there is a good reason why I am behaving the way I am, then I will come out.'

Effective trading decision-making: visualizing the possibilities

Having examined the trade from the perspective of upside expectations, Martin Burton then examines it from the downside. All along, his aim is to ensure effective decisions are made, gauged by how he feels about the changing position.

'I then do the reverse and work out how I am going to feel if in five minutes' time the price has fallen a certain percentage. If it falls 5 per cent for no particular reason than sentiment, in another five minutes would I buy any more? If I would not buy any more, then I have probably got too many already. While I am not prepared to average, I ask myself "at what level would I be prepared to average if I wanted to average?"'

By asking himself at what point he would average, Burton is trying to determine the quantity of stock with which he would be comfortable. Again, it all comes back to being at ease. If he would be prepared to average, then he would be willing to buy some more at the current lower price. This would show he still had faith in his original analysis. This is a useful mental technique. It ensures you keep an open mind about a position and do not become fixated with a view or closed to the possibility that you may be wrong.

'How am I going to feel when I am a certain amount of money down, and I realize it is not counters but money? What you have to work out is, when that price is at a different level from where you want it to be, what are you going to be doing? Are you a buyer or a seller? You will want to be one of those two things at that level. So you work out what you want to be doing before the price gets to the other level.

'Once I have worked this out and tested myself to how much pain I can take, then if the price does go there, it is like a company accrual; you have already taken it into your books. Since you have accrued that loss, you are at ease and prepared if it occurs.'

Burton uses a military analogy to reinforce this point.

'If I was a general and sending 5000 troops into battle and suddenly the first or second line of my advance lost a couple of thousand troops, am I likely to retreat? If I believe I am not going to get wiped out if I continue to advance, because I have had early losses merely from skirmishes, then I am going to advance. If I believe I am going to think "how am I going to handle those losses?" then I should not place a trade.'

> *'How am I going to feel when I am a certain amount of money down, and I realize it is not counters but money?'*

This kind of planning is reminiscent of the advice of Sun Tzu in *Art of War* (1994) (edited by James Clavell): 'The general who wins a battle makes calculations in his temple before the battle is fought. The general who loses a battle makes but few calculations beforehand. Thus, do many calculations lead to victory, and few calculations to defeat.'

'Once you are sure you can totally handle everything that can be thrown at you, then you know you are mentally tough enough to handle it. You have to know how you feel and whether you have the strength to continue because that is the right thing to do. So you need to know in trading how you are going to feel when the share price is where you do not want it to be.

'I follow trading as if it were life – it isn't. I conduct trading as I conduct my life. If you enjoy making decisions in other aspects of your life, then you do not look at decision-making in terms of the questions being asked of you; you look at it like a chess-pawn being put towards you. You ask yourself, "if I move my pawn there, then what happens to the other positions on the board?" And you go through the moves as if it were on a chess board.

'There is a level I can think through and am comfortable with when I am making the trading decision. It is because I have already made the decision of positioning moves that are going to come against me that I am relaxed about what I am going to do.'

Burton adopts a useful technique to focus on his trading actions and to prepare for all eventualities. He thinks ahead and puts himself in the possible positions he is likely to encounter. This technique can be very useful for when one of the eventualities occurs and you have to make a tough decision. Mental rehearsal in advance can lead to more efficient and effective execution. I cannot emphasize enough the usefulness of this technique. 'What do you think will happen, and if it does, what will you do?' As Martin Burton acknowledges, 'in everything you do in trading, you are being tested. But you are also mentally testing yourself. When the position you are in goes against you, you are being tested as to how you are going to react.'

> *'You need to know in trading how you are going to feel when the share price is where you do not want it to be.'*

If you find it difficult to cut your losses, then before you enter a trade you should visualize it going wrong and hitting a target at which you have promised to exit. Next, picture yourself exiting.

Repeat the exercise until it feels like second nature. Similarly, if you often find yourself taking premature profits, picture the stock hitting a price level at which you would not sell and picture yourself not selling and reasoning why.

Think in terms of price and time

Remember, your mental rehearsals have to take account of both price targets and the time it takes to achieve them. It is no use to you if your target of a 2 per cent price rise is achieved six months later, when you were looking to exit the trade in a week.

'Now the thing that comes into play is how quickly the stock price changes. If it does it immediately for no apparent reason, then obviously you will have worked out what you are going to do in that situation. If it drifts there over a few days, you may be more concerned. So you work out not only the levels but the time it takes to get there. So it is not just a question of picking levels as the mechanical traders do; it is also a question of the time-span in which it gets there. That is critical. You know that if it drifts away from the target, then you will be more worried than if it quickly overshoots away from the target because of a big sell order. A big sell order is not a reason to panic but a reason to buy some more at the cheaper price.

'If I have anticipated a 10 per cent rise but I get a 5 per cent rise with little risk, it may very well be that I take that because there was very little effort involved in that. I might think it rose 5 per cent because of a technical shortage and so it has over-reached itself in the time-frame I had in my mind, and is not going to go higher in the time-frame I am considering.'

Martin Burton evaluates his targets in the context of time, always remembering that the shorter the period he is in the market for a given gain, the better.

Focus on the method, not on chasing the market

Like everyone else, Burton's ultimate goal is to make money. But he knows that in order to do that he has to focus on his preparation and mental work. Therefore a loss is still a success if he does what he had planned to do. He measures success, not by how much he could have made if he had behaved differently, but by whether or not he did what he planned.

> *'I am totally at ease with cutting out a position too early that I am at unease with.'*

'I have no problem if the price goes up a further 5 per cent after I have sold it and reaches my original expectation. It is irritating. But because I have traded within myself I am happy if I make money or if I don't because I have done the preparation work in my mind.

'If I am trading within my own method and thought process, then if I have sold my position out before I should ever have done so, fearing it could be a loss, and it turns out to be a major profit, I just turn my back on it. It makes no difference to me. I am totally at ease with cutting out a position too early that I am at unease with. What I do fear is saying I am going to do something and not doing it. Like not taking a position which I told myself I was going to do. Believing that with my ears pricked I should have been frightened and then for some reason disobeying my instinctive fear – that irritates me.'

Your trading system is your trading plan; an indicator of what you should do and when you should do it. Traders must maintain confidence in their systems. On the voracious seas that are the markets, your system is the one thing you can hold on to. If you let go of your system, you will be lost. If you trade by the 'seat of your pants', you are assured consistent losses peppered with a few successes but it is only by sticking to a well-prepared plan that you are assured consistent successes peppered with only a few losses. That is one reason why Martin Burton ensures he does what he has planned to do. Doing what he planned to do is always the right decision for Burton, and is always a decision without regrets.

'You just have to make sure that you make the right decision when you have the loss. The key thing when you are down is to make sure you have no regrets and you will not have regrets if you make the right decision. And you will make the right decision if you have pre-thought it through. If I had a motto in life it would be that I do not ever want to regret anything. That does not mean you cannot take losses or cannot do things that are wrong, it just means if you do them and it turns out to be wrong, then you did it because it was your decision. You did not do it because it was spontaneous.'

It is easier for Martin Burton to make and execute his difficult decisions because he knows the game is not over in a day.

'As for selling something which turns out to be profitable, that is not an issue. You have to be at ease and I am at ease. It is not a 90-minute game. You have to come back. You do not have to score today. There will be a game tomorrow. There will be a game every day if you want to play. You do not have to worry about that position; you can play tomorrow. It is there whenever you want to play. So do not get hung up.'

The perspective of the great traders is hugely different from that of almost every other trader. They do not need to focus negatively and unconstructively on what could have been, because they know this was not their final shot. The game goes on. For instance, you do not get upset and think (for too long) about what could have been if your lottery numbers had come up today. It is that 'forget it,

'If I had a motto in life it would be that I do not ever want to regret anything.'

we'll play next week' attitude you need if, after exiting a position, you see it rise. Concentrate positively on the future and not negatively on the past.

A new view on losses

Most traders hate losses. They hate them so much that they often deny their existence by switching off their computers and not opening letters from their brokers. That is denial. The most famous example of trader denial was the placing of losses in a 88888 account. Great traders view losses very differently. Great traders are not aggressive, go-getting perfectionists, after everything they can get their hands on, who are desperately cut-up if they miss the slightest opportunity.

'The characteristic which I believe works for me is that I believe I am reasonably well-balanced. I am not academic but I have a high degree of common sense. I enjoy as much as anyone the successes, but I can be reasonably humble about my losses. I am more than happy to acknowledge my losses. When you have made as many as I have you probably need to acknowledge them.'

If you are not to suffer from denial and paralysis, you have to acknowledge your losses. One of the best ways to acknowledge and accept your losses is first to admit them. Secondly, recognize that the game goes on and on and on. You can always play. A loss is not a total loss but a blip. Indeed, as Martin Burton goes on to explain, a loss need not be a loss at all. As Roth (1933–) said in *The Great American Novel*, 'The sooner we get of losing, the happier everyone will be'.

'I found every increased loss of benefit because if you lose £500 then the next time you lose £450 it is not a mental problem. So each time you are in a better position to make a decision. You need to realize it is not that important when you have taken those losses.

'You have to make sure any decisions you make you are happy to live by. Accountability is very important, both in life in the way you act as a person, you are accountable to your family and friends and colleagues, and you are accountable to your trading position. It is just a case of making sure you are strong enough to be accountable. You have to be accountable and not regret. In order not to regret you need to be able to pull the trigger.'

Great traders will view a loss as a success, but only if they did everything they were supposed to do – if they acted as their system told them. In that case, they ought then to have no regrets. Define success and failure in terms of whether or not you stick by your system through thick and thin, and do not define success and failure by the losses you incur. With this shift in focus you will find the profits take care of themselves. Of course you have to keep your eye on the ball, but you first need to know where the ball is.

Independence and self-belief

Martin Burton recounted a story which merits recounting because it exemplifies traders' need to stand up courageously to the crowd and do what they feel is right. This is something which may sometimes lead you to suffer a loss, but more often it will lead to profits and renewed self-confidence.

'We were alerted to the fact that we were about to enter the Falkland's war. In response to the government announcement I spoke to a couple of Army officers as to the type of conflict we were about to embark on. Universally they said to me although the conflict was as the papers were predicting, it was not in any way as straightforward as the papers were predicting. I identified there would be plenty of scope for disappointment in this conflict. I decided to be short on every share in my portfolio of shares. The thing that I had not taken into account was the time it would take our forces to arrive at the Falklands. I was the only one at our company who was short. Each day there was the old adage you do not sell a war. It took three weeks via Ascension Island for us to reach South Georgia.

'The immediate impact was a walkover of the entire island and each day my bear had crept up. I was under the pressure of my peers and my short position. I believed in my position, nevertheless the peer pressure was great. Sure enough, it turned out we would be relatively unscathed. However, serious doubts had crept into the minds of the market and political community for a few days, especially when we started losing ships, and at that point the market had started dropping sharply. All that happened was that I was able to recover my losses. Although I didn't make any money, I did not lose any either.

'That was memorable because I felt unpatriotic. I was doing a job. I was a professional trader and was not one of the crowd. I do believe that through my trading there is a degree of contrary thinking. That was a painful process and I had serious doubts as to what I was doing as a trader.'

As a great trader you need to be resolute in your decisions yet flexible enough to re-evaluate. It is not an easy task. On the one hand you need the stubbornness of courage, and yet also the open-mindedness of wisdom. Such judgment comes only with honesty with yourself. You have to ask yourself why are you doing what you are doing. If you still believe your analysis to be correct, then do not allow yourself to be moved. However, you must also regularly re-evaluate the situation in light of new information to ensure your position is still correct. The captain of a ship does not set his course and then promptly go to sleep; he maintains a look-out. To paraphrase Kipling, 'you must trust yourself when all men doubt you, but make allowance for their doubting too'.

TRADING TACTICS

- How do you feel? Should you trade given the way you feel?

- It is all right not to trade.

- Does your trading style suit your personality? If not, change your trading style.

- What is your profit expectation for this trade?

- How long do you expect it will take to realize those expectations?

- How will you feel if the price falls 5 per cent in five minutes?

- Plan how you will react to the various possible outcomes.

- Do what you planned to do and the money will take care of itself.

- Trading is not a one-shot game. You can play tomorrow.

- A loss is a success if you followed your system.

- Believe in your decisions, but maintain an open mind; no one said it was easy.

8

Paul RT Johnson Jr

'I ENJOY IT, ESPECIALLY
WHEN I MAKE MONEY.'

TRADING TOPICS

- Types of trading fear: missed opportunities, succeeding, losing

- Trading discipline

- The desire to trade

Fame is attracted to some individuals. The week before I met Paul RT Johnson Jr at the Union League Club of Chicago, he had been photographed there with Tom Baldwin by *Cigar Aficionado* magazine. The subsequent week, as I sat back at the Chicago Board of Trade to watch the film for visitors, there on the screen appeared Paul RT Johnson Jr to explain what his job involves. And now, in the fame trilogy, he, of course, is in this book!

Like so many leading traders, Paul experienced the markets at a young age, and that taster in youth never left him. He saw 'traders trade' while visiting the CBOT at the age of eight. Today, after a spell in the early 1980s at the Chicago Mercantile Exchange, he sits on the Board of Directors of the Chicago Board of Trade and is a floor trader. Paul is also Senior Vice President at ING Securities, Futures & Options, Inc. and President of LSU Trading Company. Primarily, he and his partners provide market analysis and trade for institutional users of interest rate derivatives such as money center banks, hedge funds and proprietary trading groups. Much of his income stems from trading for his own occount.

The fearless trader

Listening to Paul RT Johnson Jr it became clear 'great' traders – and anyone who has been in this business as long as he has and has made as much money is 'great' – view things differently from other traders. It is probably true of successful people generally. They have a different perspective, a different attitude. It is not something as simple as mere optimism. It is as if their map to trading glory is drawn with a bird's-eye view instead of at ground level. They can see the inter-connections better and their view is further. Fortunately for us, this attitude can be cultivated.

As a trader there are several types of fear you will have encountered:

- Missed opportunity fear, that is the fear of not entering a trade and missing an opportunity.
- Fear of success.
- Losing fear, that is the fear of exiting and taking a loss.

Throughout this book I touch upon their causes and the solutions to removing them.

Missed opportunity fear

Here, normal traders feel that if they do not act they are going to miss the opportunity of a life-time. They believe opportunity does not knock twice and to be successful they must aggressively grasp every possibility of success. These are admirable traits outside the arena of trading, and that is why we possess them. We are brought up to believe these things. But they spell doom for the successful trader.

> *'I would rather miss a trade than lose money.'*

What works in life is often not what works in trading. That is why people who have been successful in other walks of life often fail to become successful traders. The skills they have learnt to achieve success elsewhere will actually often accelerate failure in trading. Great traders have an entirely different viewpoint.

'There is always another day. That is what many people forget. Some of the smarter guys realize that there is another day, and those are the guys that leave in the morning. They have found their niche. I was talking to one guy this morning – he had had a great day, was at work 20 minutes. Got in, got out. He felt that in a quiet market he cannot trade.

'In the pits I think you have got to be a little aggressive. It is an intimidating atmosphere out there. You can't be afraid. I think to be a trader at all you have got to have an attitude that you are not afraid of things. Because if you are too tentative you miss too many trades. It is okay to miss trades; I would rather miss a trade than lose money. If you miss it, you miss it. There will be another one along in a minute.'

The fear often materializes because a trading plan, with clear entry and exit signals is not being followed. The trader is tempted to trade on whim, or to use a perceived ambiguity in the trading plan in order to 'get some action'. For example, traders may have a rule whereby they will enter a trade if the three-day moving average crosses the ten-day moving average. But if they do not have a rule as to what to do if the two moving averages touch but do not cross, then when the two moving averages touch they will enter the trade without waiting a further day to see if the moving averages cross. The pressure to trade can be reinforced if traders have not traded for a while, or have losses to recoup, or worst still need the money.

To eliminate this fear you need first to remove all extraneous irrelevant considerations. After all, you never made a profit because you *needed* to make one. The best way to remove irrelevancies from your thought processes is to focus on your trading signals. Write down as objectively as possible the market signals that suggest you ought to trade and the ones that suggest you ought not to trade. Then concentrate on these alone and block out any other tempting thoughts.

Unlike in life, to be successful in trading you have to neutralize the 'missed opportunity fear'. In order to do that you will have to remind yourself that what works in life does not work in trading. Remind yourself that in trading, to be successful means waiting for just the right moment. If everything does not feel right, then do not play. Be overcautious. If you wait, you will be rewarded. Moreover, unlike in life, there is always another opportunity around the corner.

Fear of success

You may find this hard to believe but a lot of people are subconsciously afraid of success. All the better for the rest of us you might think – unless subconsciously you are one of them and do not know it.

'I think the fear of success is much greater than the fear of failure.'

'I believe there is a fear of success within a lot of people. I have a dear friend that I grew up with who was a fireman. He literally blew the job after he got it. He got everything he had always wanted all his life, yet he found a way of blowing it.

'There is a pressure which comes with success; people expect you to keep on doing it and you fear "what if I can't do it again". I think the fear of success is much greater than the fear of failure on the floor.'

How do you know if you are afraid of success? Well, ask yourself the following questions:

- Do you become apprehensive about commencing a new venture similar to the one you have just completed?
- Do you wonder about the negative aspects of completing a project?
- Do you feel the weight of expectation on your shoulders from friends and colleagues?
- Do you hear yourself saying 'do I have to prove myself again?'
- Do you give yourself a 'break' after a successful trade or do you jump right in to trade again?
- When you are making money trading, do you suddenly find the time to trade decreases and all of a sudden you become busy?

Of course some of these are not technically manifestations of the fear of success, but they are closely related. To neutralize this fear, you must first attempt to recognize why you believe it exists. Is it family expectation for instance? Next you have either to remove the cause or to neutralize the effect. Neutralizing the effect can be done through a recognition of the problem combined with a determination to overcome it. Remind yourself of the benefits of success. Say to yourself you want the success. Condition yourself through picturing trading success and verbalizing your desire to succeed.

Losing fear

In life generally a fear of losing can be a good motivator for success. In trading, however, it can be your undoing. In trading it manifests itself as the fear of taking a loss.

Imagine you have a position which shows a loss. You ignore the old maxim, 'cut your losses short'. Then very soon the losses increase. You are tempted to ignore them. You try to pay less attention to the losses. You become too busy to concentrate on them. You promise yourself that now you only want to break even on the position and not even make a profit.

As the price slides lower and lower, your promises change to 'getting out at the slightest rise in prices'. Every time you remember the loss you feel tense and annoyed. Occasionally, you verbally abuse yourself for being so useless. You sometimes remember your past failings; 'maybe you are a loser', you think. Maybe you are being punished, so desperately you try to think what the lesson is you are being taught. Soon there is a price bump, and you think it may be a reprieve, a turn of luck. Maybe you should hold on and try to break even after all? But soon thereafter, the price drops to its lowest level yet. Now you are blaming yourself and the market. The market knows your position and it is out to get you. Each time you think of the loss your head feels heavy and your body hunches over. You are swamped in misery. Next time you say you will not make the same mistake twice. If there is a price bump, you will definitely sell. The price bump never comes. Or if there is a bump, you get out. Looking back you realize you could have exited at a slight loss many days ago. As you calculate how much money you could have saved you get angry and frustrated.

Even worse, soon thereafter the price soars and, instead of thinking that you should have exited earlier at the slight loss and entered again at the low point, you think you should never have exited at all. You learn nothing from this experience, and like humanity, you eagerly await the next opportunity to repeat your mistakes.

If this has happened to you, then you need to change your attitude and perception of losses. There are several points you need to know to avoid making this mistake.

It is all right to be wrong

You may have read or heard this before. You probably did not want to accept it. 'Sure, it's all right for everyone else to be wrong, but not for me.' A change in mental attitude cannot come about unless the new attitude is strongly imprinted into the mind. It is not Alpesh Patel who is telling you that it is all right to be wrong in trading, it is Paul RT Johnson Jr. Paul RT Johnson Jr, a Director of CBOT, gives you permission to be wrong. Martin Burton, the Managing Director of Monument, gives you permission to be wrong. Phil Flynn, the Vice President of Alaron Trading, gives you permission to be wrong. Every trader in this book gives you permission to be wrong.

'Guys like Richard Dennis will tell you that he will make 95 per cent of his money on 5 per cent of his trades.'

The greatest psychological barrier Paul Johnson had to overcome in trading was 'to say that I am wrong, that I am fallible. I have a fear of failure and looking like I am a failure. Being wrong is something you have to come to terms with. You are going to be wrong. You are not perfect.'

When I asked Paul Johnson what his greatest trading characteristic is, he didn't say it was aggressive competitiveness, or the innate intuitive ability to recognize there is money to be made, or even the ability to pile into a trade and make a killing. He simply replied: 'A confidence to know I am wrong. It is okay to fail occasionally. I suppose most traders can't. The turnover at the exchange is like a new business, you come and you go. And often it seems to me it's because you couldn't say you are wrong, and eventually you were forced to.' Remember M.H. Alderson's observation, 'if at first you don't succeed, you are running about average'.

> **'You are going to be wrong. You are not perfect.'**

Don't get headbeam fixation

When a rabbit is about to cross a road in the dead of night, occasionally it will catch sight of two bright hovering orbs growing larger. As the accompanying rumble reaches a crescendo, the rabbit remains fixated. Humans can be like rabbits in this (and other) ways. A trader will become fixated despite knowledge of impending doom. Be aware when you are in a losing position. Be aware or be a rabbit.

'There are guys who don't want to look at the newspaper, they don't want to know the numbers, because it screws them up. Then they have a preconceived notion of where the market is supposed to go. All of a sudden they will think it is supposed to go somewhere and then they can't do what they should have done and they lose.'

The lesson is to avoid getting fixated. For some they get fixated, that is they do not follow their system when they read the papers. That is unusual. For most the fixation is with tips. They hear a tip, and start ignoring their system. Avoid, evade, ignore – do whatever you have to do in order to steer clear of getting fixated. Focus on the other side of the road and get across it.

Focus on the system, not the outcome

Part of the reason it is so hard to cut a loss is because we lose sight of what we are supposed to be doing. We are supposed to be obeying our trading system. Great traders focus on their system and let the profits take care of themselves; poor traders focus on the outcome and let the system take care of itself. Your system should be such that it indicates exits while losses are still small. As Paul RT Johnson Jr explains, making losses small means keeping bigger profits.

'We realized that we could add significantly to the amount of money we put into our pockets if we take the small losses. Take a lot of small losses instead of the big losses. I remember many times in the past I would be right eight times in a row, and lose it all in the ninth trade.

'I don't mind being wrong. I have been wrong over and over again. It is when I wind up not cutting my losses, invariably that is what gets to me. Whether it be an ego thing or whatever. Then you let them run, and maybe double up and then you blow yourself up. If you take a loss, then I think you have to understand you are going to have those. They are minor. You have to take those in your stride.'

What Paul RT Johnson Jr is discussing is that taking a small loss, according to your system, will save you a lot of money compared to focusing on the size of the loss and ignoring your system. So you have to ensure that your system indicates when to get out while still showing a small loss. Examine your trading system as objectively as possible. Write down all the relevant considerations and *only* the

> 'Many times in the past I would be right eight times in a row, and lose it all in the ninth trade.'

relevant considerations. The written word provides an excellent point of focus.

'I will look at technicals and fundamentals and say "okay, this is what is happening". I know then whether I am right or wrong, and should be adding to my winner or taking from my loser. Just take that loss and stand back. 'Okay, you blew it. Stand back and re-evaluate.'

As well as exiting a losing position when your system tells you to, you also need to exit when the original reasons for your entry no longer apply.

'As the position grows you get more and more cautious. If I am short 100 bonds, I step back and think how I would do it if it were literally a one lot and play those parameters. But you are constantly looking for what is moving the market and what could change. A lot depends on why you have the trade on. If you are long because you think the market is going to go up, you make sure that is the trade you have on and you go with it.'

What Paul is discussing is that when the original reasons why you placed the trade no longer apply, you should get out. Everything turns on your system. That is why it is so important to have defined clearly your reasons for entry; they will, to a large extent, define your exit. It is only on the rare occasions that you would stay in a position despite the original reasons for entry (for example, an annual report) weakening. For instance, unforeseen information (a take-over bid) may cause a favorable price change and your original reasons for entry no longer apply, but it makes sense to keep the position on in light of the new event.

> **'Okay, you blew it. Stand back and re-evaluate.'**

Another major reason we find it difficult to take a loss is because we fear that the position may turn around after we have exited. This is another manifestation of the fear of losing. But again you should focus on the outcome and not the system. This is just like the 'missed opportunity fear'. Again, you have to remember that you cannot see into the future. If you want to ignore your system on the basis that the loss may turn around, then you are simply gambling on the basis of hope. That is your prerogative – it's your money.

'You don't know if you are closing a losing position that may go back up. You can only go by the rules you have set for yourself, what you believe is in front of you. If it is trading at your stop, then you have to go with it. It is one of the biggest emotional mistakes I make. You just have to stick with what you know.'

'I think if you are looking back to learn, then that is always a good idea. If you are looking back to punish yourself, then you are some sort of masochist. That is true in any part of life – learn from your mistakes. My father always told me to learn from the things he did right and the things he did wrong and just don't do them.'

> **'You just have to stick with what you know.'**

When you start defining your success in terms of how well you applied your methodology instead of your outcome, you will be more in control of your trading and your trading life. The more you feel in control, the better your trading will become.

'I would almost look at it as a success that you have taken this loss. You met your parameters and you moved on. It's when you have 50 of those in a row that you get worried.'

What Paul calls 'moving on' is very important. When you are sitting on a loss you expend a lot of psychological and physical energy. You are anxious, frustrated, angry, annoyed. All these emotions detract from the clear, cool-headed thinking needed to trade effectively. Sitting on a loss has many hidden costs; one of them is that it causes you to miss trades you would not otherwise have missed. Once you cut a loss and move on, you can relieve yourself of these negative emotions and free yourself for the next opportunity.

Beware the slow market

Just as you may open a position you should not have opened, because you feared missing an opportunity, there is also the danger of opening a bad position out of sheer, plain old boredom. The 'itchy finger syndrome' has taken many dollars to their trading graves.

'That's a lot of guys' problem. That is also why a lot of guys leave early or at certain times. Because if you hang around the quiet market, you get bored and you start buying when you shouldn't. But there are guys who love slow markets. A good friend of mine, one of the largest spreaders on the eurodollar pit, loves slow days, makes his money on the slow days. We all just need to know what markets we should trade.'

The key is to recognize the market environment and then be comfortable with it. Ask yourself the following questions:

- Is it a slow market? Are there any reports coming out? Is it a short week? Is there a holiday due?
- If so, from what you know about your trading system and your personality, are you suited to trade in a quiet market? To profit, does your system need big market moves?

If you or your trading system are not suited to a quiet market, don't hang around. If professional traders leave after 20 minutes, then you should have no problems doing so. In fact it would be a sign of professionalism; you have identified a problem and avoided it.

Trading is no time to be a rebel

Avoid excuses, excuses, excuses

As Paul RT Johnson Jr explains above, not cutting your losses is part of a bigger problem – not following your trading rules. Your trading rules may be to pre-define your losses before entry, to not 'beat yourself up' if something goes wrong. When faced with a loss, even though we have clear rules, it is surprising how often we do not follow them. Why? The human mind has a great capacity for rationalization, excuse and justification to enable the body to do what is comforting. Sitting on a loss rather than cutting it can be comforting.

'You wouldn't break your rules unless you had convinced yourself somewhere in your mind that it was the right thing to do. More times than not when you break those rules you know you shouldn't. I might end up talking myself into selling when what I should do is stay with it. I should realize I have screwed up and not make it any worse.'

So you need to be aware that even with a clear system you may be tempted to sleep-walk to disaster by making self-comforting excuses why you should not cut your losses.

Good intentions and the path to salvation

You will have gathered by now that successful trading requires the discipline to follow a trading system. Many would-be great traders fail because they lack the self-discipline needed to follow their system. Paul Johnson believes you can improve self-discipline.

'Go to boot camp and join the marines for a little while. The other way is sit down and talk to yourself and analyze where you are losing. I am not a big believer in psychologists, they seem to have more problems than the rest of us, which is why they can understand them and proves they can't solve them.

'You sit back and analyze what you have done. Realize how you have broken whatever rules there are. Go in with a better idea of how you are going into a day. Many times I lose money when I get reckless and realize I am wrong but you stay with it. But that is when I get emotional, with a "let it ride" attitude.'

As well as checking yourself to make sure you are not feeling careless before you trade, you also need to keep a note of your rules in front of you, and whether and when you are breaking them.

'I think you need to sit down and write down the rules you have. If you sit down and write down what you are trying to accomplish and where you are failing, and take a list of the things you are doing wrong and the list of the things you are doing right, then work at correcting the things you are doing wrong and add to the things you are doing right.

'I think you have to have self-analysis, especially if you are not succeeding, to work out why. Take a look at yourself. It is like anything. If you are building a puzzle at home and the pieces don't fit together – why? Use a different piece. Or change the puzzle. Because you *can* change the puzzle. You *can* change the way you trade, or your outlook.'

Therefore you must identify what it is you have to do (the rules) and the possible reasons why you might not want to do it. Reasons you may not want to do something may be that you feel lazy, you are scared of change, you do not believe you can do it, etc. Once you have identified the possible reasons why you may not want to do something, list the benefits of doing it. For example, the benefits may include making more money, proving to yourself that you can achieve goals you set your mind to. Finally, affirm to yourself these positive reasons. Write them on a card. Each time you feel you may be losing some self-discipline, pull the card out and focus on the positive reasons for doing what needs to be done. But remember, affirmation without conviction is too weak to effect change. You have to really want change.

A lack of self-discipline often arises from an internal conflict. You do not want to do something, and that is why you need the discipline to do it. After all, what discipline is required to do something you enjoy? For example, if you have 'trigger fear', you will often find excuses for not doing a task you truly know you should do. You will procrastinate and rationalize. Recognize this in yourself and you will have become aware of where in your trading you need self-discipline.

'If you are doing everything right, do not analyze anything. Leave it alone. Sometimes it may mean you need a vacation. For some guys going through a divorce they can't make money. For some people they need that focus. So sometimes it could be something in your personal life and you need to step away.'

To summarize:

1. List your rules.
2. List the rules at which you procrastinate before implementation.
3. Ask yourself, and list, why it is you do not want to implement those rules.
4. List the benefits of implementing those rules – the more benefits the better.
5. Focus on the benefits.

Finally, remember, lessons such as these take time, often a life-time to learn. Only on your last trading day will you know if you failed.

'I certainly hope I am not as disciplined as I am going to be five years from now. We have to keep learning.'

Love it, to improve at it

A key factor in trading success is the love of the game. Whenever you enjoy or are passionate about any activity the likelihood is that you will excel at it. The task becomes easy, yet remains interesting and challenging. You look forward to it. It almost becomes an obsession. Your enthusiasm and confidence feed off each other.

'But I enjoy it, especially when I make money. I can't see, unless I destroy myself somehow, that I will give it up. It is immediate gratification. There have been times when I have thought I should call it quits. But I found that being away I missed it. You tend not to pay attention when you don't have a financial stake to keep your interest. So from that standpoint I always wanted to be involved, even if just to make sure I had my finger in the pot.'

A passion for trading comes largely from motivation. With many things either you are or you are not motivated. It is possible to give motivation a helping hand. Ultimately, every trader's motive is to make money. First, you need to list the intermediate goals you will have to achieve before you reach this ultimate goal. For instance, your intermediate goals may include being more disciplined, cutting short your losses efficiently and effectively. Secondly, you need to focus on the benefits of achieving these goals. This could include financial security, independence, the ability to retire. Now you have a focused source of motivation. Over time this should become more and more tangible, so it becomes a source of commitment and enjoyment.

> *'Confidence not cockiness.'*

'Motivation is one of the biggest things. You have to be motivated to make money. You must not let winning large or losing large affect you, other than to give you the confidence to trade larger and larger. Confidence not cockiness. Some people can grow forever, some people can't. It depends on who you are.'

Reduce excess stress

Stress can be a hindrance to effective motivation. It can get in the way of enjoyment. Stress needs to be managed. Shoulders are sometimes needed for leaning on. But also remember Paul's advice:

'No, I do not think stress is a bad thing. Some of the times when I knew I have had to come back, I have had some of my best weeks, because my focus has been that much greater. My wife is a great life partner who also has a business and does very well. I wonder if sometimes I lose my focus because of that.

'People will tell you stress in trading is greater than any other job, but it depends on who you are. You know you are wrong right away, so there is the stress of dealing with that. But there is stress in everything. Sure, there can also be that financial stress; the stress of losing everything.

'I probably do better with less stress. It is when you start to doubt who you are that you add stress to yourself.

'There are times when you find you have to kick it into gear and that motivation becomes a little bit greater. For me, I feel I am not succeeding like I should and I kick it up.'

As Paul notes, stress is double-edged. It can provide an extra motivation – the flame under the posterior. It can also be debilitating. Stress needs to be managed, not feared. Identify the sources of trading stress, and go back to basics. If you are stressed because of losses, then read the sections on losses and re-evaluate.

What is the one thing I should do to improve?

I asked Paul this question, since I have been asked it myself many times.

'You should probably study psychology rather than math to trade, unless you are trading options in which case math is probably more important. That's probably why Tom Baldwin is so good – he's a psychology major, he knows when and why people are sweating and how they are likely to behave.

'You have got to understand what is going on around you. Somebody asked me today "what should I study before I get into trading", and I said, "psychology". You don't need to know the intricacies of economic data, because there are so many people around you who analyze it and tell you what it means. If you are going to look at it and try to analyze it, then you are too late anyway.'

Paul RT Johnson Jr sees technical analysis and price charts as a manifestation of psychology. Your understanding of psychology is particularly important if you are a technical analyst or floor trader. The next time you examine a chart, try to picture the mental processes of the traders who produced those chart patterns. 'Wasn't that breakout the

'Human nature repeats itself, history doesn't.'

product of increased bullish determination to defeat the bears and then a subsequent round of short covering as the shorts realized they had lost the battle?' Or, 'when a price opens at its low and slowly climbs to its high during the day, is that not a sign of ever-increasing bullish confidence and ever-weakening bearish confidence?'

'Charts tell you how people have reacted to prices. Whether they form head and shoulders or wedges, it is said this is how they have reacted to those levels and when they have traded prices this way they become extremely worried when it crosses that neckline. What's the old saying, "Human nature repeats itself, history doesn't." That's what the charts are – they are human nature.'

TRADING TACTICS

- Identify missed opportunity fear, the fear of success and losing fear.

- It is better to miss a trade than to lose money.

- Opportunity does knock twice in the markets.

- Recognize, then neutralize, the fear of success; focus on the benefits, not disbenefits, of success.

- Beware of getting 'itchy fingers' in slow, boring markets.

- It's all right to be wrong; your success depends on admitting it.

- Be aware of headbeam fixation.

- Focus on performing well according to your system, and do not focus on the profit/loss outcome.

- Taking small losses means keeping big profits.

9

Brian Winterflood

'I AM THE MOST
FORTUNATE BLOKE YOU
WILL EVER MEET.'

TRADING TOPICS

- Trading motivations and goals
- Working at succeeding
- Self-belief
- Responsibilities of a trader
- Attachment to positions
- Cutting losses
- The market as a source of information

Winterflood Securities (WINS) was established in May 1988. It provides a jobbing service (creating and providing dealing prices) in over half the companies quoted on the London Stock Exchange, the complete list of AIM (Alternative Investment Market) stocks, 90 per cent of SEAT stocks, plus the whole of the Gilts Market. It is now a subsidiary of the Close Brothers Group, the second largest 'quoted' Merchant Bank. There are only three major wholly English Houses left in London: BZW, NatWest Securities and Winterflood Securities.

As we spoke, Brian Winterflood would occasionally glance through the glass panel in the door which led to the dealing floor. The dealing floor had some two dozen dealers and traders. Brian Winterflood remains the Managing Director of WINS at the age of 60. Despite his age, evidenced by his brilliant white hair, he has more energy, enthusiasm, passion and vision than most 25 year olds. He has been in the City for around 44 years. There are few men that can speak with the same authority of experience. This chapter offers not only an insight into the mind of a trader but also an insight into the mind of a man who has achieved immense success.

A history of Brian Winterflood

'I started off my career in 1953 in the City at a stockbrokers, Greener Dreyfus & Co, as a messenger and then I did National Service [compulsory military service]. When I came back from National Service in 1958, it was quite obvious that unless you were born with a silver spoon in your mouth, you weren't going to make any money and things really were very difficult. I decided that there was an opportunity on the other side of the fence – to become a jobber. As a jobber you were considered as good as your abilities. So I came over the fence and became a jobber's clerk and then a blue button and so on.

'We ran a business on the partners' capital really, and performed an important part of the Stock Exchange function. Jobbers worked only as principals, as opposed to the broker who was on the agency side. My original firm was Bisgood Bishop. In the final analysis coming up to Big Bang we were number five in the big five, although, I have to tell you that number five was a long way from number four.

'So, although we were tiny, we were still in the top five and of course we were courted by lots of merchant banks and clearing banks because of the scarcity of market-makers. You see, you needed three parts to be in the securities industry. You needed a bank, a broker and a market-maker which then became an integrated house, which we became under the wing of County NatWest.

'It was a terrible time. It was all about greed and avarice, the industry had got everything wrong. Dealers on reasonable salaries, overnight got huge salaries. What people did not understand at these integrated houses was that jobbers were risk-takers. This was their justification – to put up their money and take a risk. Obviously, in the culture of merchant banks and clearing banks, risk-taking was an anathema. I left County NatWest in 1988. It was not a very nice situation there and I walked away and then started WINS.

'I am rather proud to go about the City of London telling everybody I meet that I am the last jobber. Everybody else is an integrated house. We have no product here, we give no advice, we only provide a first-class dealing service to the retail trade and to the institutional trade on the net dealing basis. At the moment we are a niche player. We are a jobber and our claim to fame is in relation to the smaller companies and in that we provide a first-class service.

'The only motto out there is that if the telephone rings more than twice before we answer it, then we will be considered a Mickey Mouse outfit. So we are very efficient, we do make sure we answer the telephones quickly and we ensure we provide a first-class dealing service.'

In fact I found another motto, which was placed on a side table in Brian Winterflood's office: 'We have no strategy, no philosophy, no concepts. We are pragmatic opportunists' (Michel François-Poncet, Chairman and CEO Paribas).

Playing the game has to be its own reward

Money alone is not enough

Getting into trading is easy; you call a broker, sign a few papers to open an account and then place your first trade. The entry barriers are exceptionally low. Many people enter this business believing that they will make money, suffer only the occasional small loss, and be happy ever after. Perhaps it is a sobering thought then that very few individuals at even the largest investment banks in the world are allowed to place proprietary trades (trades on the company's own behalf, usually with a view to direction). Even proprietary traders have to go through years of training before they are set loose. When they are allowed to proprietary trade they are monitored very closely – usually.

> *'If you get up in the morning and don't want to come to work then you are in the wrong job.'*

The hope of making money will not provide adequate motivation to succeed in this business. Hope can only take so many knocks before it evaporates, taking motivation with it. To last in this business, to persist in the face of losses, to be committed despite being wrong, to hold on despite debts, requires something more powerful than hope. To truly succeed you need a love for what you are doing and a passion for doing it. Brian Winterflood is unequivocal in expressing his views on the subject.

'I say to people here, if you get up in the morning and don't want to come to work then you are in the wrong job. I have never had a day when I did not want to come in, even to the extent of canceling holidays it's magical and wonderful . . . wonderful.

'Everybody has got to have something to look forward to, something to attain, and it can't just be money. When you are struggling to come along, you are trying to make money just for the sake of making money. But you've got to have a longer and wider horizon I think. I know lots of guys who do have those horizons, they're here, there and everywhere.

'In hindsight, I can't think what else I would ever have wanted to do. I love the people business. I think if I ever did anything other than this I would probably have gone into PR. I like marketing this company.'

So, how can you fall more in love with what you do? There are a variety of techniques:

1. List and then focus on all the aspects of trading you like.
2. List the negative aspects of trading. Can any of these be mitigated? For example, if you hate reading company accounts, perhaps you could consider technical analysis, or a news service that summarizes and interprets the contents of company accounts.
3. Are there any positive aspects to the negative aspects – any silver linings – that you could focus on?

Another useful technique to increase enjoyment is to set goals, which I discuss in the chapter on Neal Weintraub. But, be aware. These are artificial techniques to some extent. If you do not have a natural passion for what you do, then think long and hard about why you are doing it and what else you could do instead.

A passionate affair

Brian Winterflood's passion for his work comes through from his descriptions of his old working environment. This is the pinnacle of passion; being enthralled by the smallest details, love of even the routines, enjoying things others would not notice or would have forgotten. Brian Winterflood raises his eyes above the throng and sees the beauty you can only see when not looking at the person next to you, but over his head; when you truly see. This importance of enthusiasm for achieving success was captured by H.W. Arnold: 'Let a man lose everything in the world but his enthusiasm and he will come through again to success.'

'I recall the magic of getting on that floor on day one. For instance, I remember walking up the stairs and seeing this great big bin, and light and smoke coming out of it and end-burns burning in there. Cigarettes had to go in there before we went on to the floor. A tramp would come up and empty the bin. The top hats and the bowlers were there. I also remember the magic of actually running around the City.

'In fact, I remember a chap by the name of George Lazarus. He was a big character. I don't know how to say this, but he dealt in 'kaffer stocks'; they were mining stocks. He would shout out from the top of his voice, bidding and offering stock. The whole atmosphere, the ambience, it was magical. Finally, you were allowed to smoke at 3.15pm. I smoked like a chimney. I no longer have this foolish habit.

'The waiters would come around with watering cans all day long. They had these watering cans to keep the floor damp because of the dust. You see it was a wooden floor and the dust was terrible. But you would never get wet. Another thing I remember, there was one man who would come into the Stock Exchange and into the gilt-edge market, probably once a month, and the whole Exchange would sing "Jerusalem". Don't ask me why, I don't know why. But it was great.

'I was slightly upset when giving a speech the other night to an investment club. I told them, "Well here I am tonight and I have to recall that at one stage in my career I was the youngest person on the floor in the

> *'I think you have to cram as much as you can into your mind.'*

Stock Exchange, and now I have to tell you that I am the oldest person in the group." So it has been a long career and a good career and a marvelous time and I would just like to go around again. I would go around again. I have absolutely no regrets about any of my career decisions. It has been the most marvelous career. I have no regrets. Perhaps the one regret I do have is that I never walked around the City of London on my first day and took a photograph and I never took a photograph on my first day at the Stock Exchange. Little things like that would have been really marvelous.'

Brain Winterflood's love for his work spills over into his private life. His voracious reading appetite is a product of his enjoyment for what he does.

'I read everything. There are many, many journals which are very informative. I think you have to cram as much as you can into your mind. There are very, very good magazines. Whenever I go on a journey, I take them with me. So I do become a bit of a bore on journeys.'

Do you really want to trade?

Brian Winterflood is evidence of the benefits of a positive mental attitude. All traders get a battering at times. At those times it is our attitude we have to rely upon to see us through. If you simply do not enjoy this game you are highly unlikely to succeed. Without enjoying trading, you will become frustrated in quiet markets and overtrade. Without finding the fun of trading you will be dispirited when losing, and give up. You will waste your time and money, although you may not, however, escape with your health intact. So ask yourself:

> *'Don't be scared to feel you don't know anything, because you don't know anything until you learn.'*

'Do you really, really want to do it? You have to be honest with yourself. Do you want the pressure? If you do, then you should bloody yourself straight away. Ask every question. If you don't ask you will always be one step behind. Don't be scared to feel you don't know anything, because you don't know anything until you learn. You can fill yourself with data, and get the models. I often go to lectures at the London School of Business and tell them that these models are wonderful but the fact of the matter is that they don't actually work. You get to the nitty-gritty and it's different.

> *'In the big environment it was like going to sleep at the coal face, here it is a bit like waking up at a brothel.'*

'I found a young fellow I was impressed with for our gilt operation. He knew I was looking and he came for an interview. It was quite obvious he had a lot going for him, so we took him on. He was at a major house in charge of a number of people. He said, "it suddenly occurred to me that I didn't want to get up in the morning. I wasn't enjoying going to work. I made a lot of money but there was no quality of life." An interviewer there summed it up: "In the big environment it was like going to sleep at the coal face, here it is a bit like waking up at a brothel." That sums it up.

'It was a quality of life he was looking for. He still made a lot of money, perhaps not as much as at the other place, but now he is doing what he really wants to do and giving it all he's got. He wanted to be in an environment that would make him content and happy. In a way that sums us up. We are a lot smaller, but we try a lot harder.'

It definitely helps to have support

As traders we often focus so much on the trade or the next piece of news that we forget the broader picture. We are likely to get more enjoyment and improve our trading if our minds are clear of distractions. It can help therefore to have someone to lean on at times.

'My dear wife has been with me for 40 years. She's had to put up with highs and lows from time to time. I've always regarded my wife as a marvelous back stop to have because she has never been particularly *au fait* with the business. It allowed me to blow off steam. If I went home and I had big positions, then I could bounce them off her without much argument as she wasn't in the business. So, over the years she has been a great comfort to me. I am the most fortunate bloke you will ever meet.'

Doing the hard work

Trading is hard work. Success is born of concentration and determination. As Donald Kimball, the business executive said: 'There's no place where success comes before hard work, except in the dictionary.' The old parental imperative applies: 'You have to do your homework.' As we all remember, completing homework is difficult in the face of temptation – going out with friends, taking your partner out, playing sports, relaxing. Without adequate research, technical or fundamental, without an awareness of news that can affect your trades, you will only make money through luck. If you are not rich already, I would not place sole reliance on your luck to make you so now. Brian Winterflood exemplifies the work ethic.

'It was a hard slog getting up and getting to work at 5.30am. You could not afford to do anything else. It was a hard slog going to evening classes. We started evening classes when we finished work at 6.00pm and then we finished the classes at 9.00pm. Today we give these guys time off to go to school. I don't knock it, I'm all for progress.

'Certainly, most of the contemporaries I have about me, I don't think they would ever cancel a holiday. I don't think the thought has ever occurred to them. Certainly, it is more important for them to go to the Celtic match [Scottish football] tonight than to work an extra hour. I suppose it's a different set of priorities.'

'On the dealing floor our dealers will all know their stocks, they will all know the background, they will know what news is due. They will all have done their homework and spoken to other traders and brokers and found out what they want to do. That's because they haven't got the time to think when they are buying and selling – "should I buy for this or that". They are just buying and selling having accrued all this information. It is real time and fast.'

If you are not putting the hard work into your trading, then Brian Winterflood's message is to change your priorities. You also ought to ask yourself what is it you really want to achieve?

Are you hungry for it?

While you can get by in this business with a modicum of ambition, Brian Winterflood noted that it takes hunger to be truly successful. The ingredients of ambition – to trade better, bigger – combined with an enjoyment for what you are doing can take you to the top.

'We recruited people from anywhere. However, we were the only firm in the Stock Exchange who did not recruit graduates, for no particular reason except that we did not think graduates would be hungry enough. They are hungry these days. But they were not hungry in those days, because they expected to be on the ladder straight away, and that it would all be set out for them. They were not street-wise.

'I think great traders are born rather than made. That's why you have got a lot of East End boys in the City. They are very quick and numerate. Those boys are hit and miss. They will run hard and make money, and some of them are hard nuts. That does not mean you cannot mold someone. But because he is not actually made that way, I have my doubts if he would ever get to the top. It's a bit like being a good musician. Of course, we are all born with something, we just have to find what it is.'

'We have had lots of people over the years that we picked from anywhere in life. For instance, there was one chap – he is now my son's boss [Martin Burton] – but this one chap was recruited by one of our senior partners at a garage – he was a petrol pump attendant.

'You've got to have fire in your belly. I don't want to sound conceited about it, but in my own case, had I changed firms, I would have been mega-wealthy. I mean I'm not badly off now, but I would have been mega-wealthy. My colleagues have retired and gone off at 50, but I did not want to do that. I did not want to be a little cog in a big organiza-

> *'You've got to have fire in your belly.'*

tion. I wanted to be a big cog. I wanted to achieve things not particularly under my own name, but rather through my own abilities. I was not interested in running with the herd. That may be right, or that may be wrong, but I am happy to have done what I have done, and in the way I have done it. I don't have any regrets.

'I love being in charge of this firm. I love having these people around me. But I do think you have to have that fire. However, you can only have so many chiefs; you have to have a lot of warriors, but good ones.

> *'You can only have so many chiefs; you have to have a lot of warriors, but good ones.'*

'I often think there are people you see in a company and think, "now there's a bright chap, he'll get on". He does a very good job, but why doesn't he want to come to the top? Why doesn't he want to push me off my pedestal? Why? I don't know. He gets very well paid, he's young, he's got his finger on the pulse. But he gets married and has a child and suddenly that first fit of enthusiasm, where he was going to set the world on fire, is dampened. Getting married does have a salutary effect on you. Suddenly, school fees are more important than being king of the castle.

'So, I think people who are in fairly prominent positions have had just a bit more pluck than the other guy. They did take the chance.

They could have fallen flat on their faces. But sometimes, in a business like this, they think, "well I have got all this, do I want to go that one step further?" I see that all the time in lots of firms. You need that little bit extra to want to go that little bit further. What is so upsetting is that because they won't make that break many firms bring in someone from the outside.'

Of course, Brian Winterflood is not suggesting that you must have 'pluck' in order to lead a happy life, as long as you are happy being mediocre. As he notes: 'I often think to myself, "that guy's a shoe salesman, that's what he should be, and he is happy doing that".' His point is that those who get to the top, in trading, or anything else, have to want it. Success, unlike spontaneous combustion, does not happen of its own accord. Helen Keller, the deaf and blind writer, touched upon the type of attitude Brian Winterflood is discussing: 'Security is mostly a superstition. Avoiding danger in the long run is no safer than outright exposure. Life is either a daring adventure or nothing.'

As a trader, professional or part-time, on- or off-floor you are competing to make money with the best traders that the largest banks can find. You have to ask yourself, what is your edge? How are you going to take money from the full-time professional who has been trained to do this by a team of experts and is paid to be constantly on the ball? You need that fire in your belly to go that little bit extra; read that last report even though you are tired, read everything relevant to trading. Focus on an area, say utility companies, and try to become an expert on them. So when you trade the odds are slightly better. Rest assured your competition will know all there is to know about their companies. Ultimately, you will have to ask yourself, 'is trading a hobby, or do I want to reach for the skies?' Brian Winterflood's own career is testimony to what he is discussing.

'Well actually, when I was working my way up the ladder I was very happy and content. I liked the people I was working with. There were three of us in Bisgood and it was almost like see no evil, hear no evil and speak no evil. We all went drinking together, we all did our own thing and I am quite sure we were all of a mind not to upset each other. But in the end you are all different, and in the end you can't all go along in that sort of an airy-fairy way. In the end I didn't want to go drinking with the boys every night and I did not want to do the same things they did. Rather than upset them, I decided that I was going to do something different.

'I suppose I then got my own book, while they were quite happy not to have their own book, and then I became a director. It was quite obvious I wanted to be managing director, and they may have wanted to be managing directors, but they really did not put up a fight and so I became the managing director. I wanted to run things differently, and wanted the authority to put my stamp on the company, which I did. I ran along very happily with the chairman and, subsequently, we became joint managing directors. When we went to County NatWest (and we signed away everybody's future, if you like), I felt a great responsibility for those people who had been under me. I mean I had signed the thing, and we had done the deal, but nevertheless, it was my responsibility and I was not happy there. I stayed on because I felt responsible for those people. Some of the directors left and I have never spoken to them since, nor will I ever. Because they were jeopardizing other people's careers for which they were responsible.

'Eventually I left County NatWest, and when I set up WINS it was like fulfilling what I had always wanted to do really. I was an executive director at County NatWest but eventually I wanted to go further up the ladder. But by then I would have become a very tiny fish in a big pool – terrible.

'It's something in your genes I suppose – in your make-up. My father was quite an ambitious man – he had a couple of businesses. I knew I wanted to do my own thing.'

To sum up, Brian Winterflood's success in the trading business has been due in large part to a desire to move forward and upward. As he notes, ultimately it is a question of what you want. But this business is no different from any other – success requires effort and determination.

Having the confidence to take a knock

Because the markets are so competitive you will take a knock now and again. It may be that as professional traders colleagues under stress place pressure on you, or it may be that as part-time traders your positions place you under stress. Whatever the cause, you need the resilience to battle on. You have to believe you are in the right industry and that trading is for you, in order to maintain the spirit to persevere.

'You have to have self-belief otherwise you are nowhere. You have to have a strong gut feeling. It's very difficult to tell you what that is, but I knew very early on that I had the ability to do what I was doing. I felt confident in that. Having said that, when I was a blue button we had some pretty hard task-masters. After all, it was their money we were using. They would 'f' and blind, so consequently, although you were looking forward to becoming a dealer, you also feared it like mad. My goodness how things have changed. We now have chaps at 18 who want to be authorized tomorrow, and even if they are a failure it does not seem to upset them. If we were a failure we would have been devastated.

'You were never allowed to ask a price, if you were only a blue button. You were only allowed to run messages. People would ignore you. They would tell you to 'f*** off'. Frankly, it did not hurt me. I had done my National Service. Quite obviously some people were not up to it, not because they did not have the ability, but because of the pressures within that environment. As I say, these guys were hard task-masters, and there were people in the Exchange who were obnoxious, downright disgusting. I saw in National Service how some people could not take that.

'Once you were in it, there was this gut feeling. Like at the bookies. They see the patterns of the punters, where the volumes are going. If you have not got that, you are wasting your time. So it was this gut feeling you would get while "ducking and diving", as I would say. We would be waiting for the right signals, also making sure we had read everything about the stock. You soon realize, when you are watching a television program or listening to the radio, what impact that would have on the scene. It was a question of knowing what people were thinking real time, so we could sort out those who weren't "up to it".'

While self-confidence comes from knowing you are good at what you are doing, it is useful when you have a view contrary to that held by the majority. Self-belief, confidence and courage will then be needed to stand up to the crowd, especially if the crowd can be as bad as Brian Winterflood described.

'It makes me sound rather elitist, but yes, of course it was [important to stand up to the crowd]. I don't suffer fools gladly. I don't kow-tow to people, and I always speak my mind. On occasions it may have made people a bit wary of me. I hope that people respect me, rather than fear me, for it.'

Self-accountability for your trading

As a trader, when faced with losses or whenever difficult trading decisions need to be made, there is a temptation to go into denial, to abrogate responsibility for your trading. Successful traders remain accountable and answerable to themselves for all their decisions. It is this that allows them to focus on what needs to be done to mitigate impending disaster. Brian Winterflood illustrates this through an experience from his early trading days.

'What really brought it home was when I did a really huge bargain. In those days you could trade after-hours. The boss may have gone home, but you could be doing deals at 5 o'clock, 6 o'clock – all night if you wanted to.

'I remember going home one night, and I had done this huge bargain in BMC (British Motor Corporation) A bigger bargain than I had ever done. It was a lot of shares. As soon as I had done it, it came home to me that it was not just another bargain. It was a massive overnight exposure, with all the things that can happen overnight. It was a massive exposure of millions of pounds.

'I remember thinking, "should I sit through this or what?" And I thought, "no, I have to speak to my boss". I went to him and said, "I think I ought to inform you sir that I have taken a bargain tonight which I have no particular worry about, but it is a massive exposure." And he said, "and in your judgment where is it now?" "I haven't changed my mind, I still like the bargain, but there is this exposure". And he said to me, "I shouldn't worry about it".

'Of course the next day we came in, and the bloody thing went wrong. But it didn't go terribly wrong, it just went slightly wrong. By the end of the day, I lost £30,000. But he never held it against me. He said, "this is part of learning and growing up and realizing that they are not just bargains, they are real money".

'Prior to that I was dealing hundreds of times a day, but they were bargains, they weren't real money. That experience was a real lesson. He said: "We all make mistakes, but the one thing that we are very grateful for is that you did tell us about the exposure." I found that very reassuring, but equally it allowed me to look at dealing in a slightly different way; I was much more aware of my responsibilities. It all seems very mundane now. What's happened now is that people take vast gambles without the right checks and balances. That is where you can go terribly wrong. I felt I put the whole firm in jeopardy. But people don't care nowadays.'

As Brian Winterflood explains, as traders we have a great responsibility to be open to ourselves and those for whom we work. At best only your livelihood will be affected, at worst the livelihoods of hundreds of fellow employees will be affected.

Never get attached to a position

Brian Winterflood is absolutely clear that it is wrong, as a trader, to get attached to a company. Such attachment clouds your judgment. It leads to giving too much weight to irrelevancies when deciding whether to enter or exit a position.

'At WINS, we have dealing desks of $2\frac{1}{2}$ people [each person looks after two desks and shares cover over a third desk]. $2\frac{1}{2}$ people look after 125 companies. Those 125 companies are allocated a certain amount of money, and if the dealers go beyond that, then they are fined, which impinges on their P&L.

'We can see everything because everything is real time. If they have a deal outside those parameters, they will go to the directors. What I say is, "liken your book to being a second-hand car dealer. You have

> 'Don't you tell me you know this stock is going up. You do not.'

125 cars in the forecourt. I don't mind you putting a gallon in each, but don't you dare fill up those petrol tanks. Because you can't know more than the markets. Don't you tell me you know this stock is going up. You do not." As far as you are concerned, these are just apples and pears. It is all they are. Never get emotional about a company, because tomorrow it could change. In fact we have stopped sending dealers on company visits. We send them on goodwill visits, but not company visits, because they can get emotional about a company. They see a company, they see the product, and they like the product, without considering the underlying balance sheet. So we don't like to do that.'

Losses: better to get out sooner than later

As every trader knows, there is an often irresistible temptation to sit on a loss. There is comfort in doing nothing and hoping it will come right. Brian Winterflood explains how, in his experience, it is far better to get out quick. Once you are out, you can examine things afresh and re-plan your strategy.

'What we do here is a hard-copy position, run-off every day, and that tells me all the companies we have acquired and the companies that, for whatever reason, have been hanging around too long. The catch-phrase is that "the first cut is the best cut". If you have a stock that has been on the books for more than a day, then you cut it. But the first cut is most definitely the best cut, because that allows you to start again.

'To give you an idea, yesterday we had a company which came out with terrible results. They dropped 60 per cent. We had them on our books. It cost us £25,000. But as soon as we started trading we cut, cut, cut. We forced the price down because we were cutting. Then we thought it had gone far enough, so we started buying. People were still selling, but we were buying. At the end of the day we made all our money back. So our motto is "the first cut is the best cut". Get out of it and start again; do not grin and bear it. I always say to them, "we're not an investment trust".'

'The first cut is most definitely the best cut.'

But what then if a trader is cutting out a position which may turn up again?

'He doesn't know, and he doesn't care. Why should he, because here comes the next opportunity. He is not an investment trust. He is not there to pontificate on the value of a share. He is there for price formation. It is a money operation here. You just have to get on with it.'

So, for Brian Winterflood, it does not matter what the theoretical value of the company is, and whether the current price will reach the theoretical value in the future. Your job is to be concerned with where the market is now, and deal with that. While Brian Winterflood is discussing dealers, he also means that traders ought not to let short-term trades turn into investments, where that was not the original intention.

> *It is a money operation here. You just have to get on with it.'*

The market tells you everything

For Brian Winterflood, the market is always right. There is no point arguing with the market. That does not, of course, mean that you cannot expect the price to change to a new level in the future.

'The market tells you everything. All that we do is reflect supply and demand and use our risk capital to keep continuous two-way price in operation. A stock is priced 3–6 because it is 3–6. It may be that you get a big order and sell 100,000 at 6 and think maybe they should be 5–7. But often without flow of information, they are 3–6 because they are 3–6.

'We pay no attention to technical analysis. To give you an example, when we were on the floor of the London Stock Exchange, Durlacher were standing next to us, and they are a big house. When a big report would come out it would go up on the screen and everyone would go and read it. You had to interpret it without any particular qualifications, no MBA. The way you interpreted it was to look for the right pointers. Durlacher's dealers would be on to the analyst or statistician. And these were people with experience. They would be asked their opinion, which would help the dealers to produce a price. We were the second XI. I thought, "this won't do, we've got to get the business". So I said to our chaps, it doesn't matter what Durlacher is doing. People would wait until this guy said, "oh, yes, I think the price is . . . 38". I said to our chaps, "what we've got to do is, as soon as those figures come out, to say right, is it good or bad? Don't worry about anyone else". That way we may get the first price wrong, but we won't get the second price wrong. We had the price while their analyst was still talking about it. That's the way we do business. We just said, "let's see what the market says, let us recognize supply and demand, and let us translate that into the price".'

You can also use the market to interpret data.

'We get figures and think "these must be good, even in the worst-case scenario". But there is a big bull market and people can't wait to get out, and so, despite the good figures, the price falls. Of course, there are short-term technicals. Take Barclays, whose figures weren't that good, but they said there would be a share buy-back and it went up for a day or two and then fell. That is where we make money. That is where the turnover is.'

Sometimes data will be released which you expect to affect the price. The best traders do not examine company data in isolation. They focus on the consequences of the data for the price. They then observe how the price reacts. It is the price reaction to the data that is the most important factor in deciding what the data means. Let the market tell you whether the data is bullish or bearish. The market is

> 'We may get the first price wrong, but we won't get the second price wrong.'

rarely wrong. So, for instance, there may be the release of annual results by, say, British Aerospace. Often the market-makers will have bid the stock up as soon as trading begins, if they perceived the results to be bullish and not an anticlimax. However, if most of what was announced was already in the price, the shares will drift and may well close at the day's low. It's a function of the market to sort out the day-to-day business. It usually has little effect on the ongoing price of the company's shares. Thereon after, for a little while, the shares sometimes get neglected, through lack of interest, this is more apparent in minor companies than major names. I can assure you that nine times out ten the price of the stock will drift for the next few days through lack of interest.

What has happened is that the market-makers have interpreted the figures as bullish. But throughout the day there has been selling at those high prices. As the market-makers are on the other side of this selling, they are in fact buyers. They now want to off-load this stock and the price starts to drift down to attract buyers. Watch out for a price to open at the high of the day and then drift down to close near the low for the day, after the release of company data. It is a good indicator of the market's view of the data.

TRADING TACTICS

- If your sole goal is to make money from trading, it is unlikely to provide sufficient motivation for success.

- You need to have a passion for trading. Focus on what you enjoy and mitigate what you dislike about trading.

- Ask yourself if trading is really what you want to do.

- Find people on whose shoulder you can lean for advice.

- Trading success requires hard work – never think it is easy.

- Try to maintain your self-confidence and self-belief, so you can get back up when you are knocked down. Do not knock yourself, there are plenty of people ready to do that for you.

- Traders are responsible to themselves and those affected by their trading activities.

- You should never be emotionally attached to a position.

- Losses: the first cut is the best cut.

- The market is an excellent disseminator of company announcements.

10

Neal T. Weintraub

'YOU CANNOT MASTER
THE MARKET UNTIL YOU
MASTER YOURSELF.'

TRADING TOPICS

- Stops

- The importance of motivation

- Trading goals

- Journal keeping to improve trading

- Managing trading stress

- Health for wealth

- Types of trader

Neal Weintraub is a pit trader (local) as well as an off-floor computer trader. Perhaps more significantly, Weintraub is an educator and commodity trading advisor. He is the founder of the Center for Advanced Research in Computerized Trading and conducts seminars on day trading and international hedging. Weintraub teaches at De Paul University, the Chicago Mercantile Exchange, and has been on the staff of the Chicago Board of Trade, where he was instrumental in introducing the Treasury Bond Options contract. Most of Weintraub's students are professional floor personnel and career traders, from both the US and around the world. He is also a solution producer for Omega Research.

The *Wall Street Journal* has featured his Pivot Point technique and he is frequently quoted in the trade press. Indeed, in conjunction with TradeWind Publishing, Neal has recently launched the *Weintraub Day Trader* software, which incorporates Pivot Point analysis. Neal Weintraub is the author of *The Weintraub Day Trader* (1991) and *Tricks of the Floor Trader* (1996). He is a member of the MidAmerica Commodity Exchange and clears his trades through Goldenberg and Hehmeyer at the Chicago Board of Trade. His current book *Trading Chicago Style* will be available from 1998.

During my day with Neal Weintraub, I went to his office, clearing firm, health club, and even a seminar on trading he gave at De Paul University to a group of Thai students. By the end of the day I had amassed a wealth of information and we decided that the need for an interview had been circumvented. Consequently, the contents of this chapter are based on the events of that day and the materials Neal gave me. Additionally, I have also referred in small part to Neal's book, *Tricks of the Floor Trader*, which is a much overdue book on what occurs on the floor and from which off-the-floor traders can benefit. Rightfully, the book is in its third print run and is published in German and Chinese.

Using stops properly

Throughout *Tricks of the Floor Trader* Neal discusses the use of stops in various contexts. Almost all of what he says is known only to a select few.

Newsletter stops

There is money to be made in publishing trading newsletters – that's why there are so many of them. When recommending trades, most newsletters place stops so that readers know when to close a position. Usually the stops are placed around the most recent highs or lows. According to Neal, traders at the Exchanges read these newsletters and note where members of the public are placing their stops. The floor traders will send their clerks to the Exchanges' libraries and have them note the stops. The floor trader uses the stops, not to exit, but to enter a market.

> '*The floor trader uses the stops, not to exit, but to enter a market.*'

Stops as a way of entering a falling market

This also deals with using stops to enter a market. At 7.43am on 20 July 1996 the September D-Mark was making new highs and traders' fingers were getting burnt as they tried to pick the market top. As the D-Mark traded 6823, Neal analyzed that if it broke support at 6800, it could nose-dive. He placed an order with his floor broker. 'Sell 1 September D-Mark on a sell stop at 6803.' The D-Mark broke, and Neal's order was filled at 6800. The market continued to fall and Neal bought his position back at 6686 at 10.48am.

Using this type of order to enter on a stop, the trader ought to be aware of a few points:

- It should only be used in highly volatile markets.
- Breakouts should be anticipated.
- A stop becomes a market order, so you may get filled quite a few ticks away from your stop, depending on volatility.
- Be very careful in a fast market.

Trading without stops

Neal notes that, in his experience, one reason traders lose is that their stops get hit, and then the market rallies back to their original target. Commercials trade without placing stops. Neal notes that one way to trade like a commercial is to trade with options. He cautions, however, that that is the only time not to use stops. Essentially, one buys calls when the commercials are long futures, and buys puts when the commercials are short futures.

The advantages of options over futures in this regard is that, in the futures market, not only do you choose the direction of the market, but you must be right in the price you choose to enter (or risk hefty margin payments). With options, there are no margin payments required if the price goes against you before returning in the direction you had anticipated. Essentially, there is less pressure to get the entry price precisely correct.

Running stops

Large traders often hit the bids of locals and then force them to cover. The scenario goes:

What's the bid? (Large institution asks local)
60 bid, sell you 10, what's the bid?
55 bid, sell you 20, what's the bid?
50 bid, sell you 30, what's the bid?
45 bid, sell you 40, what's the bid?
40 bid, sell you 50, what's the bid?

So the locals have been buying and the market has been forced lower by the big trader selling. Now the trader who was selling starts bidding, '45 bid', then '50 bid'. All the locals who sold at 45 and 40 are now trying desperately to get out. Meanwhile your computer screen shows a stock that is plummeting and a possible sell signal. This roller coaster leaves you out of the market, and somewhat frustrated.

The importance of motivation

'Lacking motivation is not as bad as not knowing we lack motivation.'

Too often thinking about motivation is neglected by the novice trader. Because motivation stimulates and directs behavior, it has often been described as the incentive to travel the road to our goals. It is the 'why' whereas goals are the 'what'. Lacking motivation is not as bad as not *know-ing* we lack motivation. In the latter case, we will already have set off unprepared down the road to ruin, because self-knowledge will not have informed us that we lack the necessities for reaching our destination.

In trading terms, when we know what motivates us, we are in a better position to develop a system which works for us. An under-standing of motivation permits a better 'fit' with a trading system. For instance, if you are put off longer-term investments, then it is fair to say that they do not adequately motivate you. That will provide an indication of the types of trade you ought to be looking at and, in turn, the contents of a trading system that is, and is not, suitable.

The first question which needs answering is: Are you aware of what motivates you to trade and to continue to trade? Write down the answers, you will need them later. For some people the motivation to trade stems from a desire to be in control of their own destiny, a need for independence. Such individuals are not greatly attracted to the security of employment. Another common motivation for traders is to be recog-nized as self-made. Most traders rely solely on themselves for success. For others, the motivation stems from a desire to amass money and 'make it'. These individuals seek recognition, from themselves and from others.

Goals

The importance of goals

Motivation and goals go hand in hand. Motivation is the engine, and goals are the destination. Motivation cannot exist without goals, and goals cannot exist without motivation. Each loses meaning without the other.

Setting goals provides direction to the trader. Remember Tom Copeland's words: 'You've removed most of the roadblocks to success when you've learned the difference between motion and direction.' With a series of goals traders have something on

> 'We first plan where we want to be. Only then do we consider how we are going to get there.'

which to focus and direct their energies. We can see the trees despite the wood. Focus in turn leads to more productive actions, and less wasted time and energy.

Goals are the first stage of any plan. We first plan where we want to be. Only then do we consider how we are going to get there. Setting goals also decreases anxieties, because we have a better idea of where we want to be.

As we start achieving our goals, we develop self-trust, confidence and a positive attitude. I have lost count of the number of times traders in this book remarked on the importance of those traits for trading success.

In order to generate trading goals:

- think first about the motivations you listed above. As Neal says in the *Tricks of the Floor Trader*, 'you cannot master the market until you master yourself'
- think about what you need to do to achieve your ultimate aim
- consider what is stopping you achieving your aims
- what price will you have to pay to achieve these goals? Are you willing to pay it?

The answers to these questions will assist in generating your goals.

How to set trading goals

In order to be effective, trading goals need to have certain properties:

1. They need to be specific. That means you need to define them clearly and precisely. Otherwise they will be blurred and ambiguous and you will have little hope of being able to focus on them.
2. They have to be measurable. In other words, trading goals need to be quantitative and qualitative. If you cannot measure how you

have improved, you can lose motivation. Similarly, if you cannot measure how you have not changed, you cannot concentrate on areas where you have not improved. To write that you 'want to make a lot of money' is not a productive motivational goal. However, they should not be all or nothing. You should set for your goals an optimistic, realistic and 'need to improve' target.

3. The goal needs to have a time-frame. A goal without a time-frame provides little impetus for achievement, for there is always tomorrow, or the day after, or the year after in which to achieve it. Having a time-frame tells you when you have to start traveling, and how quickly you need to go. Furthermore, your trading goals themselves need to be divided into short- (daily), medium- and long-term goals. Breaking your journey down into smaller destinations along the way is an excellent way of reaching your ultimate destination. The achievement of each smaller goal provides an impetus to continue through providing a reward for your perseverance.

4. Effective trading goals need to be realistic. This is one of the most common failings of traders. If you have never traded options, then your first goal has to be to read a certain number of books on options, options trading and options strategies. If your goals are unrealistic, they will lead to frustration, anger and ultimately a lack of motivation.

> **'To write that you "want to make a lot of money" is not a productive motivational goal.'**

5. A trading goal needs to be as much in your control as possible. It is far less likely you will arrive at a destination in the gift of others.

6. They need to be stated positively. In other words, do not state what you wish to avoid, but rather what you wish to do. So, for instance, instead of saying, 'I will not add to a losing position', you should write, 'I will limit my risk in a trade to $1000 or 3 per cent of my total capital'.

7. Goals need to be both performance and outcome oriented. Performance goals relate to success defined in terms of improvement over yourself and the mastery of skills. Outcome goals relate to a specific profit.

8. In order to avoid being overwhelmed with the number of goals you have written down, the next thing to do is to rank them, or categorize them. In other words, break them up into smaller groupings.

9. Finally, keep your goals at hand. Do not write them down and file them away. Pin them to a wall where you will see them daily, but do not let them become stale recitations.

Monitor your goals

Your goals needed constant monitoring. Adjust the difficulty of your goals. If you have difficulty in achieving them, amend them. If they are too easy, make them more difficult. It is up to you to be your own trainer. But be realistic. You will not make 1000 per cent on your money.

Journal-keeping for trading improvement

Why journal-keeping is important

I am regularly asked by traders what they can do to improve their trading. One of the easiest and simplest steps that can be undertaken is to keep a journal. Imagine all that information and experience you collect as you trade. Without a journal you are throwing so much of it away. Without a journal you are in serious danger of repeating your mistakes. In this regard, keeping a journal is a money and risk management technique. By identifying possible trading problems, you can start to resolve them. So, make journal-keeping a goal.

What to record in your journal

1. You will want to have a copy of your goals, and note your progress in achieving them.
2. The anatomy of every trade. Write down, from the moment you started analyzing a stock to the moment after you sold it, how you felt at each key moment about every activity you undertook. You may want to compare that with what you know about how you should have reacted, in light of what you have read in this book. For example, how did you feel as you approached your stop-loss?
3. Write down what feels good and what feels uncomfortable about what you are doing.

Remember to keep your notes clear and well presented. You will have to return to them at a later date.

The holistic trader

One of the major differences between good professional traders, and non-professional traders is that the former do not view trading as separate from the rest of their lives. They work to ensure all aspects of their lives support each other and are in harmony. To this end, Neal Weintraub believes in the importance of good health and stress management to trading well.

Stress management

Stress can assist or detract from your trading. Much depends on how you react to stressful situations. Do you view them as a challenge, a learning experience, or an opportunity to shine? Or do you view stressful situations as a time when you are cornered, with few choices, and out of control of your own life?

Below are some questions. The answers will provide you with some idea of how 'stressed' trading makes you. That self-knowledge can then be used to avoid the consequences of stress and improve your trading.

1. Does your personal life get affected by your trading experiences?
2. Do you frequently think about failing?
3. Do your moods change in parallel with your trading performance?
4. Do you want to totally change your trading system?
5. Do you find it difficult to concentrate?
6. Do you find it difficult to 'switch off'?
7. Are you paying less attention to your trading system?
8. Do you find you hear but do not listen to what others are saying?
9. Are you becoming more forgetful?
10. Do you feel tired and wanting to sleep all the time?

Reducing trading stress

Your answers to the above questions will have given you an indication of how stressed you are. The next issue is to deal with that stress and reduce it. These are some suggestions – take them seriously, they are on the path to greater trading success.

1. Diet. Consider a balanced, low-fat diet and regular meal times, reducing caffeine consumption.

2. Aerobic exercise at least three times a week. Chemicals produced in the body during exercise reduce stress. Also, a fit individual is better able to cope with stress.
3. Practice meditation, yoga or relaxation.
4. Keep a journal of your goals (see above).
5. Keep a network of support – friends and family.
6. Use breaks to do different things – to get out of the rut. For example, go to different places for lunch.
7. Get six to eight hours sleep each night. If you have difficulty sleeping, go to bed nine hours before you need to get up, that way even if you do not get to sleep straight away you should still have at least six hours sleep.
8. From your journal, identify areas that are causing you stress. Is it the size of trades or managing the number of trades? If so, resolve the situation by returning to your 'comfort zone'; cut the size of the trades or the number of open positions at any one time.

Like achieving any goal, reducing stress takes a commitment. You will need to devote time and patience to reducing stress, but remember that that time is being spent on improving your trading. You are waging a war, by other means, on poor trading. Finally, remember the words of William James, the philosopher and psychologist:

> Man alone, of all the creatures of the earth, can change his own pattern. Man alone is the architect of his own destiny. The greatest discovery in our generation is that human beings, by changing the inner attitudes of their minds, can change the outer aspects of their lives.
>
> *Pragmatism*, reprinted 1991.

Health and wealth

During my visit to Chicago, Neal showed me around the opulent East Bank Health Club. As Neal says in his book:

> Before you dive into the psychological aspects of trading and blame your poor trading on lack of discipline, develop some type of exercise program. Most emotional decisions are made when traders lack sleep. They tend to make irrational trading decisions that endanger a good trading plan. If eating the richest, most fattening food is your way of celebrating a good trading day, your next trading day will be a disaster.
>
> (*Tricks of the Floor Trader*, p. 40)

> *'If eating the richest, most fattening food is your way of celebrating a good trading day, your next trading day will be a disaster.'*

As Neal rightly observes:

> Any seminar that offers cocktails, pizza, or promotes cholesterol-laden foods does not know the importance of nutrition and trading. At our seminars, we try to encourage a visit to the East Bank Health Club in Chicago. In fact, part of our seminars are held there. Look at the best and most successful traders in the business. Most look healthy.
>
> (*Tricks of the Floor Trader*, p. 40)

Trading types

There are many types of trader. An awareness of the varieties allows you to avoid the pitfalls.

The disciplined trader

This is the ideal type of trader. You take losses and profits with ease. You focus on your system and follow it with discipline. Trading is usually a relaxed activity. You appreciate that a loss does not make you a loser.

The doubter

You find it difficult to execute at signals. You doubt your own abilities. You need to develop self-confidence. Perhaps you should paper-trade.

Blamer

All losses are someone else's fault. You blame bad fills, your broker for picking the phone up too slowly, your system for not being perfect. You need to regain your objectivity and self-responsibility.

Victim

You blame yourself. You feel the market is out to get you. You start becoming superstitious in your trading.

Optimist

You start thinking 'it's only money, I'll make it back later'. You think all losses will bounce back to a profit, or that you will start trading properly tomorrow.

Gambler

You are in it for the thrill. Money is a side issue. Risk and reward analysis hardly figure in your trades. You want to be a player, want the buzz and excitement.

Timid

You enter a trade, but panic at the sight of a profit and take it far too soon. Fear rules your trading.

Do you notice any of these characteristics in your journal? If you do, then you need to focus again on your motivations and goals. Incorporate goals to ensure actions which avoid the pitfalls listed above. For instance, if you find you are behaving like the timid trader, then you need to make it a goal that you will only close a position if your signals indicate you should. If you find you are a blamer, then a daily goal has to be to focus on what you did in a trade and how you ought to have placed the trade according to your system.

Some last(ing) advice

In my conversations with Neal Weintraub, it transpired that by coincidence we both have the same piece of poetic advice on our desks to assist our trading. This, then, is the piece of advice with which Neal Weintraub wanted to leave the traders reading this chapter.

If

If you can keep your head when all about you
Are losing theirs and blaming it on you
If you can trust yourself when all men doubt you,
But make allowance for their doubting too;
If you can wait and not be tired of waiting,
Or being lied about, don't deal in lies,
Or being hated, don't give way to hating,
And yet don't talk too good, nor talk too wise:

If you can dream – and not make dreams your master
If you can think – and not make thoughts your aim;
If you can meet with Triumph and Disaster
And treat those two impostors just the same;
If you can bear to hear the truth you've spoken

Twisted by knaves to make a trap for fools,
Or watch the things you gave your life to, broken,
And stoop and build 'em up with worn-out tools:

If you can make one heap of all your winnings
And risk it on one turn of pitch-and-toss,
And lose, and start again at your beginnings
And never breathe a word about your loss:
If you can force your heart and nerve and sinew
To serve your turn long after they are gone,
And so hold on when there is nothing in you
Except the Will which says to them: 'Hold on!'

If you can talk with crowds and keep your virtue
Or walk with kings – nor lose the common touch
If neither foes nor loving friends can hurt you,
If all men count with you, but none too much;
If you can fill the unforgiving minute
With sixty seconds' worth of distance run,
Yours is the Earth and everything that's in it,
And – which is more – you'll be a Man, my son!

RUDYARD KIPLING 1910, reprinted 1991.

For a copy of Neal's newsletter please call him on:
Phone: 001-312-407-6025, or fax: 001-312-407-6050

TRADING TACTICS

- Note newsletter stops as a possible point of entry instead of exit.

- Stops can be used to enter a market once the price has broken a support level.

- Options are a good trading vehicle if you wish to trade without stops.

- List your motivations for trading.

- You must have trading goals in order to be successful.

- Generate your trading goals, thinking about your motivation, and what you need to achieve your aims.

- Trading goals need to be specific, time-framed, measurable, realistic, stated positively and prioritized.

- Keep your goals at hand and master them.

- Record your trading experiences in your journal, so you can learn from them.

- Identify the causes of stress and make a commitment to remove them.

- Maintain a health program; it does affect your trading.

Conclusion

In this chapter I seek to provide a concise reminder of the key points mentioned time and again by the interviewees. I have not sought to provide here a condensed version of every piece of advice given in the book – that would be repetitive and not do justice to the advice given. To get the most from this chapter I would recommend you read it and each of the chapter summaries together.

While all the traders worked in different product fields, using different time-frames and different financial products with which to capture their trading ideas, they operated within the boundaries of certain common traits. The most important thing you could take away from reading this book is the attitude of the top traders to the market and their role in relation to the market. Each of the sections below captures a part of that attitude.

Trade selection

Ease

For every trade you make you should have clear in your mind the reasons for making it. You should know enough about what you expect to occur to ensure that you are comfortable with the trade and the position. Several of the traders spoke of being comfortable or at harmony with oneself when trading. They feel uncomfortable if the position feels too risky or too large. If you are not at ease, you should not be in the trade. It would be kindergarten-level trading advice to say that a trading plan is a prerequisite to trading with ease.

Planning

The top traders tend to select 'triggers and targets' to their trades. They do not trade by the seat of their pants. Planning is definitely a key aspect of trading success, in terms of clear and unambiguous 'what if' scenarios, even for the floor traders who have to react almost instantly. They try to think in advance what to do in response to each probable eventuality. Planning thereby reduces anxiety and increases confidence, and places the trader at ease, the major benefit of which is clarity of thought and an enforced discipline. The plan also eradicates hopefulness and ensures the trader stays focused on the original reasons for entering the trade.

Trading style

Because it was important to be 'comfortable' with the trades they had opened, the traders were very keen to ensure that they had a trading style suited to their personality. This affected whether they used options, futures, stocks, technical or fundamental analysis, spreads or outright positions, long- or short-term trades. Comfort in trading means traders are in a better position to achieve greater success.

Viewing open positions

Honesty is the key here. You must be aware of the mind's ability to 'kid itself'. You should forget the loss or profit that you may have and try to be detached, neutral and unemotional. View the position without hope but only reasoned expectation. Several of the chapters, particularly the interview with Bernard Oppetit, discuss ways of achieving this delicate balance.

Risk

Patience

Top traders are risk-averse. They patiently wait for the greatest reward/risk ratio. As Bill Lipschutz says, 'if most traders would learn how to sit on their hands 50 per cent of the time, they would make a lot, lot more money'. Private traders are even better able to wait patiently for such trades: they do not have someone looking over their shoulders pestering them to be in the market.

The leading traders cultivate patience because they do not have the fear of missing an opportunity. This is an important facet of their attitude to the market – that there is always another opportunity on its way. This attitude means they are comfortable not to be trading and being out of the market. This attitude also means they are at ease in taking losses and not too stressed if a loss they have taken would have been a profit if they had held on.

Funds
The source of trading funds has an important effect on trading, especially on the extent of risk you can take. So, before seeking more funds, be aware of this important dynamic.

Luck
To reduce risk, that is the operation of luck, traders try to control as much as they can. They attempt to put themselves in positions where they can be lucky, for example high probability trades with the odds stacked in their favor, so even if there is an element of luck it has a chance to work in their favor.

As both David Kyte and Bill Lipschutz note, great profits can come down to a handful of trades each year. When they feel they are in a potentially highly profitable trade, they 'push their luck', that is possibly enlarge their position and take caution not to exit prematurely. At these times they put their balls on the line.

Progressive trading
The top traders believe in progressive trading; a steady build-up of profits – not wild risks or swings at home-runs. They know that being in a position to make money tomorrow is more important than being able to make money today. Consequently, they always ensure they are never in a position where a long string of losses would force them out of the market.

Comfort zone

Top traders ensure the risk is such that they are not out of their 'comfort zones'. If they feel the risk is too great, they will cut back the position or reduce the risk by spreading. Being in the comfort zone is important for thinking clearly, making sound judgments and trading well.

Losses

Being wrong

The top traders are not afraid to admit being wrong. They do not view it as a dent to their ego. They know they will be wrong a lot of the time. They accept that and are at ease with it. Bill Lipschutz says that in currencies he would be lucky to be right 20 per cent of the time. He is always open to the possibility of being wrong. That is also why a trader needs self-confidence – to fight on and make profits.

The attitude to losses and being wrong is that it is inevitable. These traders know that to profit they have to cut losses. Losses are not an indication of being wrong, they are a necessary step along the path to profit. They view cutting losses as a pure benefit; it releases emotional energy, permits focus on future trades and means they can re-focus and think clearly again. Consequently, these leading traders view losses as providing many benefits. Indeed, many of them speak of learning from their losses. Phil Flynn even says 'learn to love your small losses'.

Responsibility

The top traders accept full responsibility for being wrong. They do not seek to make excuses or lay blame. Therefore they do not deny the losses. Even when using 'market flow' or pyramid information, they accept any ultimate decision and its consequences as their own responsibility. They accept losses and move on.

Exiting

The leading traders plan in advance what they are prepared to lose, and although this plan may be amended 'in flight', they will exit with unswerving discipline at their pre-determined exit point. There is no room for wishful, hopeful thinking, only objectivity and honesty.

For Bernard Oppetit, one exits a trade when what was expected to happen does not happen, or if what was expected does happen (i.e. the trigger). Bill Lipschutz exits if the loss is as large as he is willing to accept. That is, he gets out at a certain pain level, a point beyond which he would be outside his comfort level.

Several of the traders said success was seen as doing what one had planned to do. They focused on their trading plan and on executing their method and trading system. This avoided many pitfalls, such as chasing the market. They worried not about what the market was going to do, but rather what they were going to do in response.

Fear

Fear of a loss is good to the extent it makes a trader want to avoid losses, that is in that fear is an anxiety to maintain caution and repel arrogance. However, too much fear will affect judgment and possibly lead to trading paralysis. The leading traders maintain the fine balance partly because they accept that being wrong is part and parcel of trading and that there will always be other opportunities.

Mentors

Quite a few of the traders spoke of having mentors who had life-altering effects on them. If one cannot access mentors, then excellent substitutes can be found in magazines, internet sites (e.g. Dr J's Planet) or newsletters. One needs a mentor with a similar trading psychology and style.

Characteristics

Fascination

The leading traders are fascinated with every aspect of trading and the markets. They love what they do. They willingly think long and hard about what they are doing. This fascination gives them a natural edge. If you are not passionate about trading, your edge is reduced. However, they are not motivated or fascinated because of money – that is a by-product of their fascination. They know that money is not enough to produce great results. One has to be focused on doing the task at hand better than anybody else. This type of concentration and fascination Bill Lipschutz calls 'insane focus'. It is incomprehensible to outsiders. The enthusiasm is boundless, as exhibited by Brian Winterflood. Consequently, the tasks they undertake never feel like work.

Self-analysis

These leading traders were all self-analytical and reflective. They question every aspect of themselves: what they are doing, how they are doing it and every aspect of their trades, before and after they open them.

Tenacity

Many of the interviewees, such as Jon Najarian and Brian Winterflood for instance, exhibited a great tenacity to overcome initial failings in pursuit of their dreams. Great traders do not 'give up'.

Holistic

One of the most surprising, but in hindsight obvious, discoveries I made was that the top traders view trading as an holistic part of the rest of their lives. They need their non-trading lives to be harmonious to produce better trading results. They appreciate that non-trading stress can spill over into trading. Therefore they endeavor to keep fit and healthy, lower stress and manage all their other priorities – such as family and children – to avoid imbalances.

Trading Appendix 1

The basics of options

What is an option?

An option is a contract between the holder and the grantor (called *writer* of the option). There are basically two types: *call* options and *put* options. A call gives the holder the right, but not the obligation, to buy from the writer within a fixed period of time (the *exercise period*) a fixed quantity of the underlying security at a fixed price (being the *exercise price* or *strike price*).

For example, in the UK, '1 contract of the Barclays July 1100 calls priced at 67p' would give the holder the right to buy, any time before a fixed date in July, from the writer 1000 shares in Barclays Bank at a price of £11 each. To purchase the option in the first place the holder would have to pay the writer £670. Note that in the US equity options relate to the right to buy or sell 100 shares.

The general idea is (in the case of a call option holder) to buy shares in the future from the option holder at the fixed exercise price and then immediately sell them in the market at a profit, assuming the market price is greater than the exercise price. In the Barclays example, if the underlying price of the stock was 1200 at expiry in July, the holder would call for his 1000 shares (at a cost of £11 each) and then sell them immediately in the market at £12 each. Call holders therefore want the underlying share price to rise.

From the point of view of writers or sellers of the option, they are obliged, if 'called' upon, to sell the 1000 shares in Barclays Bank and would receive the £11 per share in return. The writers want to profit from receiving their premium, and not having to have to sell the holder any shares in the future. The call writers therefore do not generally want the market price to rise above the strike price, otherwise they will have to sell them to the call holder at a lower price than they could get in the market. In the above example, call writers would have to sell at £11 under the option, when in the market they could otherwise have received £12. Call writers therefore do not want the underlying share price to rise.

Similarly, a put option provides the holder the right, but not the obligation, for a fixed period of time, to sell to the writer a fixed quantity of the underlying security at a fixed price.

Most people trade in *traded options*. That means they can sell the option contract itself to someone else if they so wish.

How is the option price calculated and how can I profit?

The price at which an option is bought and sold is called the premium. In the above example the option premium was 67p. This is a little like a margin payment. An option's premium has two components, the *intrinsic value* and the *time value*.

Intrinsic value

A call option has intrinsic value if the underlying security price is greater than the option's strike price. A put option has intrinsic value if the underlying security price is less than the strike price. So, for example, in our above example, if the price of Barclays Bank's shares was 1110p then the option's intrinsic value would be 10p. That is, if you exercised the call, you could buy Barclays' shares from the writer at 1100p (strike price) and sell them in the market at 1110p (underlying security price). That is also why an option can never be worth less than its intrinsic value.

A call option would have no intrinsic value if the underlying price was lower than the strike price. If an option has intrinsic value, it is *in-the-money*. If an option has no intrinsic value, it is *out-of-the-money*. An option whose strike price is nearest to the underlying price is *at-the-money*.

Time value

The second component of option premium is time value. It is the difference between the option premium and its intrinsic value.

Time value = Premium – Intrinsic value

So, in our previous example time value would total 57p. Time value essentially represents the price the holder pays the writer for the uncertainty. It is the cost of risk which the writer faces. Time value erodes as expiry approaches. Therefore an option is a wasting asset in the hands of the holder.

Time value can be calculated using complex mathematical option pricing models such as the *Cox–Rubenstein Model*. The variables are risk-free interest rates, strike price, underlying security volatility and underlying security price, any dividends which would be paid if the underlying security were held.

From the above it follows that *at expiry* an out-of-the-money option is worthless and an in-the-money option is worth its intrinsic value. Note that since an option cannot have negative intrinsic or time value, the most an option holder can lose (and the most a writer can make) is the premium, no matter how much the underlying price falls.

Relationship between the option price and the price of the underlying security

The most important thing to remember is that the price of a call tends to rise as the underlying security price rises and the price of a call tends to fall as the underlying security price falls. The price of a put tends to rise as the underlying security price falls and the price of a put tends to fall as the underlying security price rises.

So why buy an option and not the security? Because an option is *leveraged*. That means that for a given percentage change in the underlying price the option price can change by a greater percentage. You get a bigger bang for your buck.

Going back to our previous example, if the price of Barclays moved from 1110p to 1150p, the option price may move from 67p to 97p. That means there would have been a 3.6 per cent change in the underlying price and a 44.7 per cent change in the option price. You could then decide to sell the option or, as before, exercise it. There would be more money to be made from selling it.

The price of an option rarely has a 1:1 correlation with the underlying security price. The *delta* is the rate of change of the option price to the rate of change of the underlying price. So, for example, a delta of 0.5 means that if the underlying price rises by, say, 10 cents, then the option price will change by 5 cents. Obviously the greater the delta then the greater the bang for your buck. However, the delta is greatest for in-the-money options, that is those with the most intrinsic value and therefore the most costly options. Consequently, a balance has to be drawn when calculating potential returns between the delta and the price of the option. An example will clarify the situation:

Barclays shares are trading at 1110p.

July 1100 calls are 51p; July 1200 calls are 16p.

If tomorrow the price of Barclays' shares were to be 1200p, then it may be that the July 1100 calls trade at 123p (average delta of 0.8) and the July 1200 calls trade at 22.5p (average delta of 0.25). The return from the July 1100s is 141% and from the cheaper 1200s is only 41%.

Of course in this example we have only estimated deltas and have ignored costs and bid-ask spreads. Nevertheless it gives you some idea of the balances that need to be drawn. For modest moves one is likely to profit most from just in-the-money options.

Strategies

Although there are only two types of options, calls and puts, there are a lot of option strategies. The simplest strategy is to go *long* a call or a put. That means you *buy to open* a call or put. If you go *short* (write the option) then you *sell to open* a call or put. In the latter case you have to post margin since your losses are potentially unlimited. It is a lot safer for the lay investor to be long puts than short calls even though on both you profit from falling prices.

Option strategies are beyond the scope of this book but I will mention a few to give you some idea of what the professionals and experienced non-professional can do with options:

Hedge A hedge is a position where one position profits if the other position loses. So a hedge can be thought of as an insurance against being wrong. For example, as a hedge against a long call, one could sell short a different call or go long a put.

Straddle Buy to open an at-the-money call and buy to open an at-the-money put. You profit by increased volatility in the underlying price irrespective of direction. The strategy is a *guts* if the options are both in-the-money and a *strangle* if they are both out-of-the-money.

Bull Call Spread Long in-the-money call and short out-of-the money call. Profit from upward price movement. This becomes a *bull call calendar spread* if the short call is nearer month than the long call.

Bear Put Spread Long in-the-money put and short out-of-the-money put. Profit from downward price movement. This becomes a *bear put calendar spread* if the short put is nearer month than the long put.

Various other strategies exist depending on one's views as to volatility and direction and extent of risk one wishes to take. These strategies have some unusual names, e.g., *butterfly, condor, iron butterfly* (buy a straddle and sell a strangle because you expect a limited size move), *combo, ladder, box, conversion,* and *reversal.*

Trading Appendix 2

The basics of futures

The most basic thing to remember about futures is that you buy them (go long) if you think the price will rise and sell them (go short) if you think it will fall.

What is a futures contract?

A futures contract has several features:

- It is a legally binding contract.
- It is usually traded through a recognized exchange (e.g., Chicago Mercantile Exchange).
- One party agrees to take delivery and the other party agrees to make delivery of the underlying asset.
- The specific *quality* and *quantity* of the underlying asset to be delivered is agreed in advance.
- The *date* of delivery is fixed in advance.
- The *price* of delivery is also fixed in advance.
- The *place* of delivery is also fixed in advance.

In other words, a futures contract is simply an agreement to deliver a specific quantity and quality of an asset at a predetermined price, place and date. If you are 'long' a futures contract, then you have bought a futures contract and so are the party that will take delivery. You may already have entered into very similar contracts; have you ever bought something and asked for it to be delivered? If you are 'short' a futures contract, then you have sold a futures contract and so are the party that will make delivery.

So, for example, a typical futures contract might look like:

Cattle (CME); 40,000 Pounds; cents per Pound, quoted at 72 for December delivery.

What this means is that each cattle futures contract on the Chicago Mercantile Exchange is for 40,000 pounds of live cattle, and prices are expressed in cents per pound. The price of 72 means 72 cents per pound. Therefore a 1 cent price move causes a $400 change in equity (i.e., 1 cent × 40,000).

Note, however, that only about 1 per cent of all futures contracts are held until delivery; they are usually 'closed' before then. That is, an equal and opposite futures trade is made which cancels out your delivery obligations. The reasons vary as to why most futures contracts are not held to delivery, but the major reason is that the futures contract is used for speculation and one does not care about the underlying asset, and also because the future is used as a hedge (see Glossary of Trading Terms.)

Futures contracts are available in hard and soft commodities, such as various types of grain and metal. There are also futures in financial products such as interest rates, currencies and indices.

Why are there futures contracts?

In the United States, between the Great Lakes and the grain-growing, livestock-rearing Great Plains, lies Chicago. A natural port for access to the world's markets for most American farmers, Chicago soon became and remains the home of the largest commodities exchanges in the world.

Picture Chicago in the 1850s. As a farmer growing wheat in rural America, each harvest I reap the rewards of my annual toils. I sell most of my wheat to a few farmers who use it to feed their livestock. Each year I pray for wheat prices to rise so that I may make greater profits when it comes to sell my wheat, and each year I worry that the prices might fall. Each year they pray for bumper crops so that the price might fall and their costs drop, and each year they worry that the price might rise. Then, while in our respective fields, it occurs to us to fix our prices several months in advance so that we may plan ahead. While we are at it, we should also fix when, where and what quality our wheat should be. What we have stumbled across is the futures contract.

Essentially, the futures contract was created to meet a business need. That need exists today – the need for certainty in an uncertain world. The futures contract permitted hedges (i.e., protection) against adverse price movements by fixing the sale price today. Of course it soon occurred to some non-farmers in stripy shirts, braces, slicked back hair and fast red Italian and German sports cars that futures could also be used to speculate.

How are futures prices fixed?

A future is a derivative. That is, its price is derived from the price of the underlying asset it refers to. A gold future's price is derived from the price of gold. The cash or spot price of the underlying asset is the price at which the underlying asset is currently being bought and sold in the market. The price of the cash asset changes with supply and demand. The futures price responds to changes in the spot price.

Obviously, at delivery the futures price and the spot price are the same. If they were not, then you could buy one and sell the other for instant profit (arbitrage). Before delivery the futures price equals the cash price plus the cost of holding the cash commodity until delivery. A little thought makes it clear why this must be so. If it were not so, suppose the futures price of wheat is high relative to the cash price of wheat, you could buy the cash wheat – store it and pay interest on the money you borrowed to pay for it – and sell ('go short') the future (i.e., promise to deliver the wheat in the future). Basically, your costs (of buying and storing the wheat) would be less than your receipts (from selling the wheat) and you would make a profit:

Price, above cash wheat price, of wheat future
per bushel for delivery in 1 month: 20 cents
Costs of holding cash wheat per bushel for 1 month   13 cents

Therefore sell the future and buy the cash stock. Deliver the cash stock against the future in one month. Locked in profit = 7 cents per bushel.

What is margin?

Initial margin is a small fraction of the contract's value paid at the time the position is opened. Variation margin is the further payments that needs to be made if the price moves adversely.

Speculation

Futures speculators are like speculators in any other asset. They seek to profit from price changes. How they come to decide what price changes are likely is their business – there as many different methods as traders. Traders may think that the UN is about to relax oil sanctions against Iraq and so the price of oil is likely to fall. As we saw before, all other things being equal, if the price of the cash commodity falls, then the price of the future is also likely to fall. Consequently, our traders may short oil futures. However, they will have to be careful that there are not countervailing price-raising forces which may swamp the effects of the UN decision. The traders will also have to ensure that the expectation of an imminent fall in oil prices is not already discounted in the price, in which case when the event eventually occurs the price will be unaffected.

Glossary of Trading Terms

Abandoned option Where an option is neither sold nor exercised but allowed to lapse at expiry.

American option An option that is exercisable at any time within its life. Can and are traded outside Europe.

Arbitrage The purchase in one market of an instrument and the sale in another market of it or a closely linked instrument in order to profit from the small price differentials between the products in the two markets. Arbitrage profits usually only exist for a small time because someone usually scoops on them since they are 'locked in'.

Arbitrageur Traders engaged in arbitrage. They seek to make a lot of small, quick profits.

Assign To oblige a call option writer to sell shares to the option holder, or to oblige a put option writer to buy shares from a put option holder.

At the market An order to buy or sell at the best price obtainable in the market.

Averaging Where a price moves against traders and they trade more of the stock to enlarge their position but to lower their overall entry price. It will mean they will have a lower exit price at which they can make a profit.

Basis point Used to calculate differences in interest rate yields. For example, the difference between 5.25% and 6.00% is 75 basis points.

Bear(ish) An individual who thinks prices will fall.

Bear market A market in which prices are falling.

Bear spread An option position where it is intended to profit from a falling market. Usually the position involves the purchase of a put at one strike price and the sale of a put at a lower strike price.

Bid An offer to purchase at a specific price.

Black–Scholes Pricing Model A mathematical model used to calculate the price in theory of an option. The main input variables are: the risk-free interest rate, volatility, dividends, time to expiry, the strike price, underlying price.

Break A sudden fall in price.

Breakout When the price moves out of its recent range. This sometimes signals further moves in the direction of the breakout.

Broker An individual who executes customers' orders.

Bull(ish) An individual who believes prices will rise.

Bull market A market in which prices are rising.

Bull spread An option position where it is intended to profit from a rising market. Usually the position involves the purchase of a call at one strike price and the sale of a call at a higher strike price.

Call option (Calls) The right, but not the obligation, existing only for a fixed period of time to purchase a fixed quantity of stock at a fixed price.

Clerk An employee of an Exchange's member firm who is registered to work on the Exchange floor.

Closed When referring to a position, this means one has made an equal and opposite trade to one already held and so has no more exposure to the market on that trade.

Contrarian An individual who generally believes it is usually better not to do what the majority are doing, because the majority do not make money.

Day trade(r) A position that is closed the same day it was opened.

Delta The change of the options price for a change in the underlying price. A delta of 0.5 means a ten-point move in the underlying price causes a five-point move in the option.

Diversification Reducing risk by spreading investments among different interments. Not putting all your eggs in a few baskets.

Drawdown The reduction in trading capital as a result of losses.

European option An option that is only exercisable at expiry.

Exercise Where the holders of an option use their right to buy or sell the underlying security. Also means to workout.

Expiry The date up to which traders can exercise their option.

Floor broker A member who executes orders for clearing members.

Floor trader Individuals who trade on the floor of an exchange either for themselves or a company.

Fundamental analysis Forecasting prices by using economic or accounting data. For example, one might base a decision to buy a stock on its yield.

Futures A standardized contract for the future delivery of goods, at a pre-arranged date, location, price.

Gap Where a price opens and trades higher than its previous close.

Hedge Protection against current or anticipated risk exposure, usually through the purchase of a derivative. For example, if you hold DM and fear that the price will decline in relation to $ you may go long $. You would then make some profit on your long position to offset your losses in holding DM.

Implied volatility Future price volatility as calculated from actual, not theoretical, options prices. The volatility is implied in the prices.

Limit The maximum permitted price move up or down for any given day, under exchange rules.

Liquid market A market which permits relatively easy entry and exit of large orders because there are so many buyers and sellers. Usually a characteristic of a popular market.

Long A position, opened but not yet closed, with a buy order.

Margin A sum placed with a broker by a trader to cover against possible losses.

Margin call A demand for cash to maintain margin requirements.

Mark to market Daily calculation of paper gains and losses using closing market prices. Also used to calculate any necessary margin that may be payable.

Market order See *At the market*

Momentum An indicator used by traders to buy or sell. It is based on the theory that the faster and further prices move in a particular direction, the more likely they are to slow and turn.

Moving average A system used by traders to determine when to buy and sell. An average (simple, exponential or other) is taken of the closing (or opening or other) prices over a specific number of previous days. A plot is made based on the average. As each day progresses, the moving average has to be re-calculated to take account of the latest data and remove the oldest data.

Offer A price at which a seller is willing to sell.

Open position A position that has not yet been closed and therefore the trader is exposed to market movements.

Overbought/oversold A term used to mean broadly that a stock is likely not to advance further and may decline (overbought) or advance (oversold).

Position Trades which result in exposure to market movements.

Put option A right, but not the obligation, existing for a specified period of time to sell a specific quantity of stock or other instrument at a specified price.

Pyramiding The increase in size of an existing position by opening further positions, usually in decreasing increments.

Scalper A trader who seeks to enter and exit the market very quickly and thereby make a lot of small profits.

Seat Exchange membership that permits floor trading.

Short An open position created by a sell order, in the expectation of a price decline and so the opportunity to profit by purchasing the instrument (so closing out) at a lower price.

Speculator An individual who purchases financial instruments in order to profit. Often used to refer to a non-professional. Sometimes used derogatively.

Spread The simultaneous purchase of one contract and the sale of a similar but not identical contract. Depending on the exact combination, a profit can be made from a rising or falling market.

Stop order (stop loss orders) An order left with a broker instructing him/her to close out an existing position if the market price reaches a certain level. Can be used to take profits or stop losses.

Technical analysis Methods used to forecast future prices using the price data alone (e.g., by plotting it as a chart and noting direction) or using the price as an input in mathematical formulae and plotting the results. Contrast this with fundamental analysis.

Technical rally or decline A price movement resulting from factors unrelated to fundamentals or supply and demand.

Tick The smallest possible price move.

Trendline A line on a price chart indicating market price direction. The line connects at least three price points which touch the line, with no prices breaking the line.

Volatility A statistical indication of probable future price movement size (but not direction) within a period of time. For example, 66 per cent probability of a 15 pence move in three months.

Whipsaw A price move first in one direction and shortly thereafter in another direction thereby catching traders wrong-footed. Such markets may be termed 'choppy'. Such effects often give rise to false buy and sell signals, leading to losses.

Recommended Reading and Internet Sites

READING

Trading psychology

The Bhagavad Gita, (translated by Geoffrey Paminder, One World, 1996.) Although written 5000 years ago, and *not* directly about trading, I found it to be one of the most useful 'trading' books I have ever read. It largely discusses discipline – how and why – and the benefits of discipline. Since a lack of mental discipline is one of the major downfalls of traders this is likely to be a very profitable read.

Mark Douglas, *The Disciplined Trader*, New York Institute of Finance, 1990. This is an extremely good book. Written in an intelligent fashion, it gets away from Mickey-Mouse fashion psychology and deserves a far higher profile than it has to date.

Robert Koppel and Howard Abell, *The Inner Game of Trading*, Probus, 1994. It includes interviews with some leading traders, but its value comes from the analysis of psychological difficulties traders are likely to encounter. It is definitely recommended.

Classics

Edwin Le Fevre, *Reminiscences of a Stock Operator*, John Wiley and Sons, 1993. An undoubted classic, this is the fictionalized trading biography of Jesse Livermore, one of the greatest speculators ever seen. While dated (it was written in 1923), it nevertheless provides some insight into the difficulties encountered by traders. A very enjoyable read.

Charles Mackay and Joseph de la Vega, *Extraordinary Popular Delusions and the Madness of Crowds and Confusiones de Confusiones*, John Wiley and Sons, 1996. This explores crowd psychology and how that affects market movement. While its examinations are 300 years old, it is highly relevant today. Short and interesting.

Futures and options

Peter Temple, *Traded Options*, Rushmere Wynne, 1995. For those trading options on LIFFE. This book provides a thorough explanation of all the basics, from what options are to buying software.

Todd Lofton, *Getting Started in Futures*, John Wiley and Sons, 1993, 2nd edn. This is a clear and easy-to-understand text as well as giving lots of information for delving deeper.

Michael Thomsett, *Getting Started in Options*, John Wiley and Sons, 1993, 2nd edn. Again, very clear and easy to understand, it is an excellent start for beginners.

Technical analysis

Martin Pring, *Technical Analysis Explained*, McGraw-Hill, 1991, 3rd edn. The first half of this book is more relevant than the second half. While a little disappointing, it nevertheless provides insights not available elsewhere.

Elli Gifford, *The Investor's Guide to Technical Analysis*, FT Pitman, 1995. While this book uses UK companies to illustrate points, it nevertheless is useful to traders in any country. Thorough, comprehensive and easy to read and understand, it is good as a starter and for more advanced study. However, it is not mathematical.

Fundamental analysis

Jack D. Schwager, *Schwager on Futures, Technical Analysis*, John Wiley and Sons, 1995.

Jack D. Schwager, *Schwager on Futures: Fundamental Analysis*, John Wiley and Sons, 1995. While expensive, it is certainly comprehensive, although confined to futures.

Peter Lynch and John Rothchild, *One Up on Wall Street*, Penguin, 1990. The stock-picking gurus provide some useful 'what to look for' rules. Written in an easy-to-digest style, it is fun to read.

Tom Copeland, Tim Koller and Jack Murrin, *Valuation, Measuring and Managing the Value of Companies*, John Wiley and Sons, 1995. This goes into some of the serious stuff. It is quantitative, as fundamental analysis should be. It runs to over 500 pages and has useful diagrams and charts.

Benjamin Graham and David Dodd, *Security Analysis*, McGraw-Hill, 1997. Another quantitative and densely analytical book. If you are serious about fundamental analysis, this book should be read.

Traders' profiles

Jack D. Schwager, *New Market Wizards*, Harper Business, 1992.

Jack D. Schwager, *Market Wizards*, New York Institute of Finance, 1989. An absolute must. Fascinating, although since it's in a question-and-answer format you are left to draw many of your own conclusions.

Kenneth L. Fisher, *100 Minds that Made the Market*, Business Classics, 1991. Biographical in nature and the profiles are somewhat short, but nevertheless a good bedtime or holiday read.

Alan Rubenfeld, *The Super Traders*, Irwin, 1992. Nine profiles of traders from diverse backgrounds. While a little bit too biographical, it nevertheless makes for a good read.

Floor trading insights
Neal Weintraub, *The Weintraub Day Trader*, Windsor, 1991.

Neal Weintraub, *Tricks of the Floor Trader*, Irwin, 1996. One of the few books of its kind, it gives the outsider a view of what the insider does and provides knowledge which is useful to know.

Grant Noble, *The Trader's Edge*, Probus, 1995. With some very useful insights into what they do on the floor, this is a good insider's view and has useful pointers on some of the advantages enjoyed by floor-traders.

William Eng, *Trading Rules*, FT Pitman, 1990. While some of the rules will be familiar, others provide valuable information, enough to justify buying this easy-to-understand book.

Economic history
The following selection provides a good cross-section of the types of book Bernard Oppetit discussed as providing an insight into how companies and consumers change.

Rondo Cameron, *A Concise Economic History of the World*, Oxford University Press, 1997, 3rd edn.

Ingomar Hauchler and Paul Kennedy, *Global Trends*, Continuum Publications Group, 1994.

Roger Bilster, *The American Aerospace Industry: From Workshop to Global Enterprise*, Twayne Publications, 1996.

Ryoshin Minami, *Acquiring, Adapting and Developing Technologies*, St Martin's Press, 1995.

Allan Kulikoff, *The Agrarian Origins of American Capitalism*, University Press of Virginia, 1992.

BIBLIOGRAPHY

Peter Bernstein, *Against the Gods* 1996.

Ralph Waldo Emerson, *Collected Poems and Translation of Ralph Waldo Emerson*, Library of America, 1994.

William James, *Pragmatism*, Prometheus Books, reprinted 1991.

Rudyard Kipling, 'If' in *Rewards and Fairies* 1910, reprinted in *Gunga Din and Other Favourite Poems*, Dover Publications, 1991.

Michael Lewis, *Liar's Poker*, Penguin, 1990.

Alpesh B. Patel, *Your Questions Answered: Money, Savings and Financial Planning*, Rushmere Wynne, 1997.

Philip Roth, *The Great American Novel*, Vintage Books, reprinted 1995.

George Bernard Shaw, *Man and Superman*, 1903.

Sun Tzu, *Art of War*, edited by James Clavell, Delta, 1988.

INTERNET SITES

News and information
Barron's   www.barrons.com

Bloomberg   www.bloomberg.com

CNBC   www.cnbc.com

Financial Times   www.ft.com

Dr J's Planet   www.drjsplanet.com
This is Jon Najarian's site. It has some excellent daily updates and trading tips.

Applied Derivatives Trading   www.adtrading.com
A free site offering a wide variety of teasingly short articles, from trading psychology to getting trading jobs. Updated monthly.

Exchanges
Many of the following exchanges send vast amounts of free information related to financial products and how they operate.

American Stock Exchange   www.amex.com

Chicago Board of Trade   www.cbot.com

Chicago Board Options Exchange   www.cboe.com

Chicago Mercantile Exchange   www.cme.com

Chicago Stock Exchange   www.chicagostockex.com

NASDAQ   www.nasdaq.com

New York Mercantile Exchange   www.nymex.com

New York Stock Exchange   www.nyse.com

London International Financial Futures, Commodities and Options Exchange
www.liffe.com

Index